P9-AER-334

BEHAVIOR MODIFICATION
Theory
and Practice

To my parents

BEHAVIOR MODIFICATION Theory and Practice

A. Robert Sherman

University of California, Santa Barbara

BROOKS/COLE PUBLISHING COMPANY
MONTEREY, CALIFORNIA
A Division of Wadsworth Publishing Company, Inc.

DISCARD

SEP 12 1977

West Hills College

616.8914
SHE

© 1973 by Wadsworth Publishing Company, Inc., Belmont, California 94002. All rights reserved. No part of this book may be reproduced, stored in a retrieval system, or transcribed, in any form or by any means—electronic, mechanical, photocopying, recording, or otherwise—without the prior written permission of the publisher: Brooks/Cole Publishing Company, Monterey, California, a division of Wadsworth Publishing Company, Inc.

ISBN: 0-8185-0066-2
L.C. Catalog Card No.: 72-85941
Printed in the United States of America
4 5 6 7 8 9 10

West Hills College Coalinga
Fitch Library
300 Cherry Lane
Coalinga, CA 93210

This book was edited by Mara Niels and designed by Jane Mitchell. It was typeset by Datagraphics, Phoenix, Arizona, and printed and bound by Malloy Lithographing, Inc., Ann Arbor, Michigan.

Preface

Behavior Modification: Theory and Practice is a brief but comprehensive introduction to behavior modification intended for use as core reading in courses on psychotherapy or clinical methods as well as supplementary reading in courses focused on human learning, personality and adjustment, abnormal behavior, or general psychology. Behavior modification involves the systematic application of psychological principles in order to change behavior in desired directions. This approach has had considerable impact in clinical and educational settings. It also makes an important contribution to scientific psychology, for behavior modification derives its principles from the more substantive areas of psychology and provides a testing ground for them. Such wide relevance has generated the need for this book.

Section 1 includes an introduction to psychotherapy and a chapter on basic concepts of learning that makes the book readable without prerequisites. Section 2 presents the behavioral treatments, including operant conditioning and extinction, imaginal and real-life desensitization, social modeling, expressive training, aversion therapy, and behavioral self-control. Descriptions of the methods and their theoretical rationales are supplemented by case studies and representative research findings. Technical and theoretical issues are discussed at the end of each chapter in an "Issues to Consider" section that will especially interest the reader who wants to pursue his understanding in greater depth. Section 3 gives an overview of behavior modification, including a table summarizing the methods and their objectives. A list of advanced readings on behavior modification, for those seeking direction for further study, is at the end of the book.

Although all major behavioral methods are covered, it should be emphasized that this introductory book is not intended as a therapy manual for practitioners: specialized knowledge and supervised training are as essential for the successful administration of behavioral treatments as for most approaches to psychotherapy.

I am indebted to several people for providing constructive criticism of the manuscript at early stages of its preparation. I am especially thankful to Dr. Edward L. Walker, Dr. Arnold A. Lazarus, and Dr. Leonard P. Ullmann for their helpful comments in reviewing the entire manuscript; to Dr. Frank D. Cox, Mr. David F. Barone, Ms. Genae Hall, and Ms. Janet Edson for their advice on selected portions; and to Ms. Mara Niels for help in editing the manuscript and improving its presentation.

A. Robert Sherman

Contents

SECTION 1

Introduction to
Psychotherapy and
Behavior
Modification

CHAPTER 1

Introduction to Psychotherapy

Everyone has had some experiences in which he felt unhappy or unable to cope with particular problems. We all know what it means to be afraid, depressed, frustrated, or inept, just as we know what it means to be relaxed, excited, happy, or competent. A wide range of performance and emotion is common to human experience. Some philosophers claim that it is necessary to have felt failure in order to fully appreciate success or to have felt pain in order to appreciate emotional pleasure. When we are experiencing personal inadequacy or emotional distress, however, such philosophy hardly consoles us. Instead, we are more concerned with what we can do to make ourselves more effective or feel better, as the case may be.

Quite often, close examination reveals that the emotional distress is related to some situation or circumstance which upsets or threatens us. For example, anticipating giving a speech in class, being rejected by a loved one, failing an important examination, being bedridden by an illness, losing a class election, and learning of the death of a relative are common experiences likely to cause some psychological stress. Ordinarily the emotional distress dissipates in a relatively short time as circumstances change, problematic situations are overcome, and new preoccupations replace them. In some instances, where the stressful situation or its recollection is either very threatening or very persistent, or where there is some personal inadequacy in a particular area, the associated distress may be severe or enduring. It is then that the sufferer may require and often seeks the help of others, initially friends and relatives, and sometimes professional psychotherapists.

The Beginnings of Psychotherapy

Seeking professional assistance for psychological problems reflects a quite different view of such difficulties from the view we had less than a century ago. Through the early part of the nineteenth century, the severely psychologically disturbed and those who occasionally exhibited unusual behavior were frequently thought to be "possessed by the devil." They were often virtually imprisoned in insane asylums—locked institutions set up not to provide care but rather to protect society from the inmates' supposedly evil ways.

By the latter half of the nineteenth century, Western society began to assume increasing responsibility for the care of those who suffered psychologically, just as it had already assumed some responsibility for the care of those who suffered physically. This new attitude toward behavioral disorders developed within the medical profession, for at that time there was no discipline of psychology. Disturbed people were no longer viewed as evil and possessed by the devil. Instead, they were assumed to suffer from some underlying mental abnormality which caused the overt symptoms of disordered behavior, just as physical symptoms (such as fever or sore throat) were generally found to indicate the presence of some underlying physical problem (infection by a virus). Consistent with this new view, physicians who attempted to help such people were concerned with identifying what the underlying psychological causes were so that these causes could be treated and the person cured; in other

4

words, this new formulation of mental illness and its treatment was based upon the *medical model.*

The Medical Model and Psychoanalysis

The medical model of behavioral disorder was most comprehensively and elaborately expressed by Sigmund Freud. Freud was medically trained in physiology and then became interested in psychological problems; he formulated a theory of personality and an approach to therapy called *psychoanalysis.* He made numerous revisions to his theories during the course of his study, which extended from the early 1890s to his death in 1939, and which produced the equivalent of about 24 book-sized volumes. During these years he also collaborated with many people who later extended his psychoanalytic formulations in new directions. Some of these early followers, as well as later "neo-Freudians," have attained prominence in their own right: Alfred Adler, Ernest Jones, Carl Jung, Otto Rank, Erich Fromm, Karen Horney, and Harry Stack Sullivan. Freud was one of the most profound influences on psychological and philosophical thought in Western society during the first half of the twentieth century.

Although we cannot consider Freud's formulations in detail, let us summarize certain basic characteristics of the psychoanalytic approach and the psychotherapeutic variations which have evolved from it.[1] As mentioned above, the Freudian approach is based on the medical model. This presumes that there are underlying causes for observed behavioral problems and that treatment must be directed not at the overt symptoms but at identifying and resolving the underlying causes. In psychoanalysis, the client is required to *free associate* —that is, to say whatever comes into his mind. What the client says and does helps the psychoanalyst understand the client's problems

[1]Many books and professional journals discuss psychoanalytic theory and practice; for comprehensive accounts, see Fenichel (1945) and Blum (1953); for briefer surveys, see Hall (1954) and Blum (1966).

and their causes, most of which are thought to be *unconscious,* or beyond the client's awareness. He also attempts to help the client share that understanding—that is, to help the client gain insight into his problems—by interpreting his impressions to the client in the hope that such understanding will promote an alleviation of those problems. Such psychoanalytic sessions often continue an hour a day for several years. This approach of seeking insight into the underlying causes of psychological difficulties is also characteristic of many other, briefer approaches to psychotherapy which have emerged since the development of psychoanalysis.

The Training of Psychotherapists

Since the beginning of the twentieth century, many professional clinicians, primarily psychiatrists and clinical psychologists, have practiced such insight-oriented psychotherapy. *Psychiatrists* are initially trained as physicians. After receiving the M.D. degree and completing a medical internship, they study behavioral disorders and their treatment through a psychiatric residency, which includes supervised on-the-job training as well as course work. *Clinical psychologists* are initially trained as scientists concerned with the study of human behavior. They learn about behavior and behavioral disorders during their graduate studies. Before receiving the Ph.D. degree, they ordinarily receive on-the-job training and do related course work during a supervised clinical internship.

Despite such different background training—the psychiatrist spends several years learning about the physical and chemical aspects of the body, while the clinical psychologist spends several years learning about theories and research on behavior—these two groups of psychotherapists generally treat their clients similarly in individual verbal psychotherapy. In practice, traditional psychotherapy tends to be somewhat unrelated to this early formal education, having little to do with the medical training of the psychiatrist or the research training of the clinical psychologist. Traditional psychotherapists are ordinarily most concerned with trying to understand the

6

causes and nature of their clients' problems and alleviating those problems by talking about them.

Behavioral Problems: Development versus Treatment

It is important to distinguish between the development of a behavioral problem and its treatment. The therapist may have a theory about psychological disorders which purports to explain the development and nature of the client's problems. However, theoretical explanations are not enough. In order to treat the problems, he must have an effective system of psychotherapy. Regardless of the validity of his developmental theory, it is his treatment approach which will primarily determine the outcome of his psychotherapeutic efforts.

Since this book is primarily concerned with the behavioral treatment of psychological problems, traditional theories of personality and personality disorder will not be described or evaluated. There is abundant literature on psychoanalytic theory, both supporting and contradicting its basic tenets. The effectiveness of therapy, however, may be evaluated independently of the theory. Even though Freud's theories of personality disorder led him and his followers to their particular treatment approaches, it is possible that their theories may be valid in certain respects while insight-oriented therapy may not be effective in changing disordered behavior.

Perhaps this idea can be clarified with an example. Suppose you find that your car's front tires are prematurely worn and that they have worn irregularly. You will want new tires as well as some assurance that the replacements will last longer. You drive to your local tire dealer, who examines your car and finds that your front wheels are out of alignment. Certainly something caused the front end to go out of alignment—perhaps it was that big chuckhole at the corner of Broadway and Main—but the manager is unlikely to be concerned about identifying the actual cause. Nor would it be worthwhile; even if he traced your auto's route for the past 15,000 miles, correctly identified the villainous chuckhole, and repaired it, your new tires would not wear any better than the old ones. Accurately understanding the original cause—even correcting it—would not necessarily resolve the current problem. However, if he repairs the overt symptoms by putting on new tires, balancing the wheels, and aligning the front end, your new tires will last longer than the old ones did (unless you hit another chuckhole).

How does this relate to therapy? Traditional psychotherapy has been described as a relationship between therapist and client in which the client does most of the talking and together the two try to understand and resolve the client's problems. This basic approach, which is most intensive and prolonged in psychoanalysis, is common to most traditional systems of individual psychotherapy. Aside from the validity or invalidity of the underlying theories, we must ask, "Do the treatments work?" Later in this chapter we shall consider evidence suggesting that traditional verbal psychotherapy may not be particularly effective in improving maladaptive behavior.

Note that such terms as *mental illness, insanity, abnormal behavior,* and *psychopathology* have evolved from the medical model with its disease orientation. As we shall see in the next chapter, the psychological model, on which the behavior modification treatments are based, does not view behavioral problems as representing illness or pathology within the person. In this view, the behavior itself is not diseased or disturbed, but it may be disturbing to the client and to others. Using the psychological model of behavior, we shall refrain from such "medical" terms as *illness, abnormality,* or *pathology,* and will instead employ terms such as *maladaptive, undesirable, disordered,* or *problematic* to refer to behaviors requiring treatment.

Problems in Evaluating Psychotherapy

The plasticity of human behavior and the complexity of its goals make precise research into psychotherapy difficult. The following outline lists some important questions related to identifying behavioral objectives, specifying treatment procedures, and assessing behavior changes. These questions also highlight issues relevant to our later survey of behavior modification methods.

Issues in the Practice and Evaluation of Psychotherapy

Identifying Behavioral Objectives

1. *Maladaptive behavior.* What is the nature of the maladaptive behavior, and what are its component features?
2. *Severity of components.* What is the relative severity of the components?
3. *Objectives and priorities.* What are to be the behavioral objectives of therapy, and what is their order of priority?
4. *Basis of objectives.* Are the objectives a function of the client's complaints, the therapist's theories, or some combination of the two?
5. *Agreement on objectives.* To what extent are the objectives stated and agreed upon at the outset of treatment?

Specifying Treatment Procedures

1. *Procedures and basis.* What procedures will the therapist use, and what is the basis for their selection?
2. *Relationship between procedures and maladaptive behaviors.* Do the procedures vary for the several components of the maladaptive behavior?
3. *Order of procedures.* What will be the order of application of the procedures?
4. *Changing procedures.* Might there be changes in the procedures as therapy progresses, and what will be the criteria for introducing such changes?
5. *Therapist characteristics.* What personal characteristics of the therapist may make him more or less suited or inclined to use particular procedures with particular clients?
6. *Client characteristics.* What personal characteristics of the client may make him more or less inclined to seek a therapist noted for using particular procedures?

Assessing Behavior Changes

1. *Measures of change.* What measuring instruments and rating scales will be used to express the extent of therapeutic change for each component of the maladaptive behavior?
2. *Weights for different sources of judgment.* What are the relative weights to be given to the judgments of the therapist, the client, the client's family and friends, and independent observers?

9

3. *Success and termination criteria.* What criteria are to be used for deciding whether the behavioral objectives have been achieved and/or for deciding that treatment ought to be terminated?

4. *Daily life influences.* How can the changes due to specific treatment procedures be isolated from those due to variable factors in the client's daily life—his work situation, marital harmony, and physical health?

5. *Interdependence with client characteristics.* To what extent are the therapeutic changes (or lack thereof) which appear to be due to specific treatment procedures partially due to an interdependence with certain client characteristics such as age, sex, and social class?

6. *Stability and durability of changes.* How might the stability and durability of the therapeutic changes be assessed after the treatment is completed, and how might such information be incorporated in the overall evaluation of the treatment?

7. *Treatment side effects.* Might there be positive or negative changes which result from the treatment procedures but to which the procedures were not directed, and how might such side effects be incorporated into the overall evaluation of the efficacy of the treatment procedures?

Obviously, the challenge of conducting precise research on psychotherapy is an imposing one. No one study can account for all relevant factors. But for some initial information in this important area, let us consider the findings of some institutions and practitioners concerning the progress of their clients. Although this is not a precisely controlled experiment, it is certainly of interest to get an idea of how effective psychotherapists think they are.

Value of Traditional Psychotherapy Is Challenged

Hans J. Eysenck, a British psychologist, surveyed the literature and published his conclusions in 1952 based on 24 reports describing over 8000 patients who had been treated by insight-oriented psychotherapy, including intensive psychoanalysis and shorter-term verbal psychotherapy based upon the medical model. He also attempted to find out approximately what percentage of people with psychological problems show improvement without any formal treatment. His findings suggested that, despite varying theories and practices, about one-half to two-thirds of neurotic patients showed marked improvement with the traditional therapies. However, Eysenck also found that the remission rate of those under custodial care—that is, without any formal treatment—also tended to be somewhere around one-half to two-thirds. If this is taken as an approximate baseline of how likely people are to show improvement without any special treatment, then traditional psychotherapies would appear to be of little value in promoting any extra improvement.

The Eysenck survey has been challenged because it was based mainly on uncontrolled outcome studies suffering from inadequate specification of the maladaptive behaviors, of the treatments employed, and of the criteria for assessing behavior change. However, since the one-half to two-thirds figure was based on independent reports of traditional psychotherapists of varying theoretical persuasions, it may be possible that the reported improvements do not result from procedures specific to any of the approaches. Instead, they may emerge from some processes common to all of them (for example, discussing one's problems with a respected person in an emotionally warm and accepting atmosphere) or from unrelated *spontaneous remission* factors (such as favorable changes in one's daily circumstances or life situation—which would be expected in any case, since the individual is most likely to seek treatment when he is at his worst). We can understand how a practitioner might come to believe in the effectiveness of his work because he sees improvement in more than half of his clients, nor is it surprising that he is likely to attribute the success to the validity of his special orientation. Eysenck's study suggests that such an attitude may not be appropriate for the psychotherapist, however, since he may in fact be adding little to the improvement which his client would have been likely to show in the absence of treatment, and what little he did add may be quite unrelated to his special theory of psychotherapy.

It is obvious that claims for the superiority of particular practices, over and above their general or nonspecific therapeutic effects, must be based upon (1) an *improvement rate* substantially above the common average, (2) an increase in the *speed of improvement,* or, in the event of practices which are equally successful and efficient, (3) a *decrease in the discomfort* to the treated individual during treatment. Even if the questionable figures on conventional therapies tend to underestimate their true values and effectiveness, there still seems much room for innovation and further improvement along each of these dimensions.

A new approach to the treatment of maladaptive behavior has evolved in recent years in response to this therapeutic challenge. This approach, based on a psychological model of problematic behavior rather than the traditional medical model, has progressively increased in scope and frequency of use; it has come to be called *behavior modification* or *behavior therapy*. The rest of this book will review that development.

CHAPTER 2

Behavior Modification: Origins and Orientation

The behavior of organisms, animal and human alike, has always fascinated mankind. In fact, a student often enrolls in his first psychology course because he is interested in his own behavior. Psychology as a scientific discipline is relatively new, however. Until the middle of the nineteenth century, most information about human behavior came from such disciplines as philosophy, religion, and physiology, and from the astute observations of insightful novelists. The primary concerns were the prescription of desirable behavior or the description of behavioral characteristics. Concurrent with and to some extent influenced by the work of Freud and his associates, observers came to note that the behavior of organisms was neither as random nor as rational as they often had presumed. Human behavior, itself, gradually came to be viewed as an appropriate object of scientific inquiry, with an increasing concern about the prediction and control of behavior. Thus was born the science of psychology.

The Beginnings of Psychology

The beginning of psychology as a formal discipline is often linked to Wilhelm Wundt, who established the first psychological laboratory at the University of Leipzig, Germany, in 1879. Wundt was concerned with the structural characteristics of conscious experience, and viewed psychology's objective as identifying the basic mental elements of which all conscious experience was presumed to be composed. This orientation came to be referred to as *structuralism*, and the method of study—which consisted of analyzing self-observations and the subjective reports of other human subjects—was known as *introspection*.

During the late nineteenth century and beginning of the twentieth century, the early history of psychology was marked by the development of several other important orientations or schools of psychology.[1] James McKeen Cattell, a student of Wundt, conducted research on human reaction time to sensory stimulation, while another scientist, Hermann Ebbinghaus, conducted research on human memory. The work of Cattell and Ebbinghaus was similar in that they were concerned not only with conscious experience, as were the introspectionists, but also with the relationship between specific external events and consequent behavior. This was the *functionalist* position, which directed increased interest toward the beginning of a new orientation in psychology: the functions of behavior and mental processes, not just their structure. William James, a philosopher and psychologist, and John Dewey, a philosopher and educator, were among the earliest proponents of this position.

The Emergence of Behaviorism and Theories of Learning

During the 1910's, psychologist John B. Watson rose to prominence; he believed that even the functionalist position was too con-

[1]For a comprehensive account of the early history of psychology, see Boring (1950).

cerned with the mind and conscious experience. Rejecting the distinction between mind and body as well as introspective methodology, he maintained instead that only observable behavior ought to be studied by psychology. This view also emphasized learned rather than unlearned behavior. Watson conducted laboratory experiments on behavior, working primarily with animals, giving impetus to the orientation called *behaviorism.*

Other important developments in the history of psychology were concerned on the one hand with controlled experimentation and theory construction and on the other hand with practical applications. Psychological testing—originating with Alfred Binet's intelligence tests and Hermann Rorschach's inkblot personality test—continues to be influential in such applied areas as clinical diagnosis, vocational counseling, and personnel selection. We have already considered the tremendous theoretical and practical impact of Sigmund Freud and psychoanalysis on the psychodynamic understanding of disordered behavior. The importance of considering the overall organization and unity of behavior, in contrast to the structuralists' emphasis on component elements, was raised by the *Gestalt* psychologists Max Wertheimer, Kurt Koffka, and Wolfgang Kohler. These and other individuals and theoretical orientations have contributed enormously to our understanding of behavior and the early development of psychology as a science. However, if one were to survey the work of American psychologists today, he would probably find that the *behavioristic* orientation is the most pervasive.

Behaviorism emphasizes observable behavior, controlled experimentation, learning, and the objectives of prediction and control. *Learning* refers to changes in behavior which result from experience. Understanding how learning occurs has been one of the main objectives of psychological researchers following the behavioristic tradition of Watson. Edward Thorndike, Ivan Pavlov, Clark Hull, Edward Tolman, Edwin Guthrie, Neal Miller, Kenneth Spence, and B. F. Skinner are among the most prominent scientists associated with the development of theories of learning. Through carefully controlled laboratory experiments with animals and humans, scientists have attempted to discover the conditions under which learning takes place and then to formulate general theories concerning the *prediction and control* of behavior. In spite of many subtle as well

15

as some manifest differences among them, the various theories generally have much in common since they attempt to explain the same behavioral phenomena. These basic principles of learning have been used to develop methods for modifying maladaptive behavior.

The Psychological Model
and Behavior Modification

The *psychological model* of behavior maintains that virtually all behavior is learned in accordance with the same basic principles. It is from this behavioristic perspective that behavior modification has emerged as an applied science for changing behavior.[2] Behavior modification derives its unique approach to treating maladaptive behavior from its foundations in learning theory; it assumes that maladaptive behavior is learned via the same principles as adaptive behavior, since both result from an interplay of genetic endowment and environmental circumstances. This means that any qualitative distinction between "normal" and "abnormal" behavior is inappropriate. In other words, the psychological model does not view behavioral problems as representing mental illness or pathology as the medical model does. Instead, it maintains that the desirability or undesirability of particular behaviors is more an attribute of the environment and the consequences of the behaviors than an attribute of the behaviors themselves. The fact that the same behavior may be effective in one situation and ineffective in another situation further illustrates this point. The appropriateness of behavior is thus viewed as a function of its adaptiveness or maladaptiveness in a particular environment rather than a normality or abnormality inherent in the behavior itself.

For example, we behave differently to our parents than to our siblings, boy friends, girl friends, or teachers. We behave differently at home than in the gymnasium, classroom, restaurant, or dentist's office. Certainly, some styles and characteristics of our behavior are

[2]For reviews of the historical development of behavior modification, see Ullmann and Krasner (1965, pp. 50–59), Yates (1970, pp. 3–19), and Lazarus (1971, pp. 1–3).

16

common to our relationships with most people and most situations, but certain behaviors are appropriate in one context and inappropriate in another. Thus, one might, in a moment of anger, tell his best friend to go to hell, but it is unlikely (or at least it used to be unlikely) that he would say the same thing to his professor when angered by a poor grade on an exam. The latter behavior would be regarded as "maladaptive" to circumstances in the psychological model, in contrast to the "abnormal" label of the traditional medical model, which presumes that there is some underlying mental disturbance causing the behavior.

Consistent with this distinction, whereas the traditional psychotherapist would try to identify and resolve underlying causes, the behavior therapist would try to identify the factors responsible for maintaining the maladaptive behavior. The behavior therapist would therefore be interested in but not too concerned with the initial manifestation of the maladaptive behavior; he would instead be interested in its inappropriateness to present circumstances. In his view, the problem is in the present, and the focus of treatment should therefore be upon the client's present behavior.

Treatment Implications of Medical Model versus Psychological Model

These distinctions between the medical model and the psychological model, and their different implications for treatment, are very important. The student's anger toward his friend and toward his professor may have been quite appropriate in both circumstances, but his common verbal response to both failed to make the important distinction between "best friend" and "professor." The traditional psychotherapist might try to find out why the student exhibited such hostile feelings toward his professor; he might try to relate this to his feelings toward his father and his general attitude toward figures of authority. Even if this analysis were valid, it would not necessarily lead to any improvement in the student's present behavior. In contrast, the behavior therapist would try to teach the student to make finer discriminations between relationships with various people. If

17

the student were found to lack skills for relating constructively with adults, the therapist might attempt to teach him more effective ways of behaving in interpersonal situations generally, and how to discuss his examination grade tactfully with his professor in particular.

This difference in the focus of treatment has often been characterized as the difference between treating the *symptom* and treating the *cause*. The behavior therapist maintains that the so-called "symptom" is the problem. He might be interested in learning about the initial manifestation of the behavioral problem—not so that presumed causes can be worked through and "resolved," but rather as a source of clues which might help in identifying the factors responsible for maintaining the behavior now. Such information might assist him in formulating a treatment strategy that would teach the individual other more adaptive behaviors for the same circumstances. The actual treatment in behavior modification, therefore, focuses upon the behavior in the present, not in the past.

The Nature of Maladaptive Behavior

Behavior therapists generally distinguish between two general classes of maladaptive behavior. First, particular behavioral responses may be inappropriate or ineffective. These are regarded as *surplus* behaviors because their presence in a particular situation has maladaptive consequences. A child who constantly calls out loudly in the classroom shows such a surplus behavioral problem. Sometime in the past, he had learned this boisterous behavior—perhaps to get attention from his parents at home or to hold his own in the playground—but now he is exhibiting the behavior in a situation in which it is disruptive and inappropriate. Another example of surplus behavior is a person who is extremely afraid of harmless insects avoiding all places where insects may be found. The objective of treatment in the case of such surplus disorders would be to retrain the person so that the problematic situations no longer evoke the maladaptive responses in him, but instead evoke more appropriate and effective behavior. Thus, the youngster in the classroom would learn to raise his hand when he had something to say in class, and the person with the phobia for insects would be taught to remain calm when he sees harmless insects.

Another kind of behavioral problem is one in which adaptive responses ordinarily learned by most individuals in a society fail to be acquired by a particular person. These are regarded as *deficiency* behaviors because their absence in a particular situation is maladaptive. A child who has reached the age of five and still wets his bed, a disorder known as "enuresis," is showing such a behavioral deficiency. He has not learned to control his bladder while asleep, whereas most children have learned this control at an earlier age. Another example of a deficiency problem is a person who has not learned to express himself well verbally in social situations, but instead relies upon gestures and mumbled phrases to communicate. The objective of treatment with both of these deficiency disorders would be to teach the appropriate responses which are missing from the client's repertoire so he can behave adaptively. Thus, the enuretic youngster would be taught to control his bladder and awaken so he can go to the toilet, and the verbally and socially inadequate person would be taught to speak and relate more effectively in social contexts.

Surplus and deficiency disorders are viewed as resulting from an interplay between individual characteristics on the one hand and adverse environmental circumstances on the other. For example, the nervous system of the person with the insect phobia may be biologically inclined to overarousal in response to novel stimuli, so that even an encounter with a harmless fruitfly might condition a fear reaction. Alternatively, his nervous system might be quite normal, but he may have developed his phobic reaction through a severe traumatic experience such as having once become critically ill as a result of an allergic reaction to a bee sting. Similarly, the verbally and interpersonally inadequate individual may have defective hearing which made it difficult for him to learn to speak, or he may have been raised in an isolated environment by an overindulgent and overprotective mother so that he never had to learn to speak in order to have his needs met and lacked experience with playmates which would have helped him to develop interpersonal skills. Often the behavioral problem is a result of factors associated with both *nature* and *nurture,* and may also have both surplus and deficiency components.

19

Preliminary Steps in Initiating a Behavioral Treatment

The therapeutic task in behavior modification is to bring about a permanent dissociation (or association) between the behavior and the environment in which its presence (or absence) is maladaptive, in a manner which maximizes the efficiency of the therapy and minimizes the discomfort to the individual. These objectives are achieved through the systematic application of carefully selected therapeutic procedures based on psychological principles derived from experimental studies.

Selecting the appropriate procedures necessarily depends upon a thorough *functional analysis* of the behavior. As part of the search for clues to help identify factors responsible for maintaining the behavior, the therapist will generally seek a comprehensive picture of the client and his life history. This may include his age, family background, marital status, personal characteristics, physical health, education, occupation, interpersonal relationships, and, of course, the nature of his psychological complaints.[3] In addition to such background information, which may be obtained directly in interviews and questionnaires, the treatment of surplus problems involving unpleasant emotions—anxiety, guilt, panic, or depression—or specific maladaptive responses requires accurate identification of the situations which precipitate these reactions. Where there appear to be behavioral deficits, it must be determined whether the requisite skills are lacking in the person's repertoire or whether their performance is being inhibited by other factors. The behavior therapist thus attempts to learn as much as possible about the client and his behavioral difficulties so he can formulate an effective therapeutic program. He is particularly interested in identifying the specific nature of the problem behavior and the characteristics of the environment in which it is maladaptive.

[3] In this general overview of preliminary steps in initiating a behavioral treatment, we are supposing the common situation of an individual adult client seeking treatment for a behavioral problem not involving organic lesions or gross psychotic features. The approach might vary with the age of the client and the nature of his complaints.

As in most systems of psychotherapy, the display of sincere empathy and the establishment of a trustful relationship are generally considered important. This is because the specific behavior therapy procedures are intended to add to the general benefits which often result from a close relationship in which one person cares about and attempts to help another person with his problems. As a preliminary orientation to the treatment, the client is generally presented with the therapist's behavioral view of psychological problems: the client's maladaptive responses are presumed to result from faulty learning experiences in the past for which he was not intentionally responsible, and any notions about an underlying mental illness or insanity are dispelled.[4] The therapist makes it clear that he will try to help the client overcome his difficulties by systematically applying certain methods based on psychological principles of learning.

After the therapist and the client have agreed on the goals of treatment, the client is introduced to the relevant behavior therapy procedures. Regarding the overall treatment plan, when there is more than one component to the problem, the client's most distressing current reactions are given priority. In behavior modification, the attempt is made to clearly specify the behavioral problems, the therapeutic objectives, and the treatment strategy, and then systematically to conduct the treatment while continually evaluating and adapting the procedures to the requirements of the individual case.

Before we begin our survey of specific methods of behavior modification, it will be helpful for us to review in Chapter 3 some of the basic concepts of learning upon which those procedures are based.

---

[4]It should be noted that this behavioristic assumption—which maintains that virtually all maladaptive behavior not physiologically based is learned in the same way as adaptive behavior—is not a proven fact. Its inclusion here is merely intended to clarify how the behavior therapist ordinarily presents the treatment to his client, the therapeutic rationale being interrelated with these theoretical assumptions.

CHAPTER 3

Basic Concepts of Learning

To understand the theories behind the behavioral treatments, we must be familiar with the terminology and basic principles of learning theory. This chapter will describe and illustrate some basic psychological concepts, with examples taken from the escapades of a little boy named Colbey. Students already familiar with learning theory can merely skim this chapter before moving on to Section Two.[1] This chapter may then serve as a reference if terms about which the student is unsure appear in the text.

> BEHAVIOR: any overt or covert activity of a person.

All areas of psychology are concerned with some aspects of behavior because, by definition, psychology is the science of behav-

[1]Students who wish a more detailed introduction to learning theory should see Walker (1967).

ior. When Colbey smiles, salivates, walks, cries, or plays, he is exhibiting behavior.

STIMULUS: an object, situation, event, or any other factor inside or outside a person that has some effect upon the person's behavior.

A stimulus may be as simple as the ring of a phone or as complex as a playing board during a chess game. In one sense, a complex stimulus consists of many smaller stimuli, but the term ordinarily refers to something *functionally related* to a person's behavior. The sight of the family car coming up the street is a stimulus which prompts Colbey to run out to greet his father returning from work.

RESPONSE: an instance of behavior such as doing something or saying something, usually involving the activity of a muscle or a gland.

A response may be as simple as an eyeblink or as complex as walking over to the phone, lifting it up, and speaking into it. In one sense, a complex response consists of many smaller responses, but the term generally refers to functionally meaningful units of behavior, such as Colbey's running out to greet father.

MOTIVATION: internal factors such as drives, needs, and interests which arouse and direct behavior toward particular goals.

A person's behavior is controlled by internal as well as external stimuli; "motivation" refers to certain categories of internal stimuli. For example, if Colbey has been playing outdoors on a hot day, he may become thirsty. If he has been deprived of water since he began playing, he might be highly motivated to go into the house to get a drink. Once he has had enough water to satiate himself, the prospect of a beverage is unlikely to be a strong incentive in guiding his behavior. In other words, his level of water deprivation influences his thirst motivation, which determines whether Colbey will go into the house to get a drink.

REINFORCEMENT: any favorable consequences of a response; includes both primary reinforcers, which satisfy basic physiological needs, and secondary reinforcers, which come to be valued because of their prior association with primary reinforcers.

A reinforcement or reward may be as simple as a glass of water or a smile or as complex as being elected president of an organization. Food and sleep are good examples of *primary* reinforcers, and money and praise are good examples of *secondary* reinforcers. What reinforces a person at one time may not reinforce him at another, as Colbey's fluctuating motivation for a drink shows. The amount of deprivation or satiation of particular rewards will therefore determine the person's motivation to behave in ways that will produce these rewards. There are also differences among people in what they find reinforcing. For example, Colbey may play quietly because his mother usually gives him a lollipop when he does. However, if Colbey's mother prepared a good dinner and Colbey's father wanted to reinforce her for this, it would probably be wiser for him to offer to take her out for dessert or help with the dishes than to give her a lollipop. One of the basic ways of determining whether something is reinforcing for a particular behavior is to see whether it increases the likelihood of that behavior recurring in the future.

LEARNING: changes in behavior resulting from experience and practice.

One of our primary concerns in behavior modification is helping people with behavioral problems learn to perform desirable behaviors and refrain from undesirable behaviors. The same principles, however, apply to the development of most of our behaviors. When Colbey pours himself a glass of water, plays quietly to get a lollipop, cries until he is picked up, or flinches when he sees someone about to slam a door, he is exhibiting learned behavior.

CONDITIONING: the learning processes through which relationships between stimuli and responses are developed.

In the above examples of Colbey's learned behaviors, note that his responses are generally associated with particular stimulus situations. For example, he might have learned to play quietly to get a lollipop when he is in his house and his mother is around. The same response of quiet play may be somewhat less likely if he were in someone else's house or if his mother were not around. Learning theory is primarily concerned with the processes by which particular responses become conditioned or attached to particular stimulus situations.

INSTRUMENTAL (OPERANT) CONDITIONING: a form of learning in which a response becomes more likely to occur in a particular stimulus situation as a result of having been instrumental in achieving reinforcement in the same or similar situations.

Colbey learned to play quietly as a result of instrumental conditioning. Although his play was occasionally peaceful, it was more often loud, boisterous, and destructive. Once when Colbey was playing quietly, his mother gave him a lollipop and praised him for "playing so nicely." The next time she noticed him playing quietly, she again reinforced him with a treat and praise. She continued to reward him in this manner, and soon Colbey's play in the house

25

became more characterized by quiet, constructive behavior than by noisy, destructive behavior. He had learned to behave in ways that paid off for him and not to behave in ways that did not pay off. Most human behavior is developed and maintained on the basis of such functional consequences.

CLASSICAL (RESPONDENT) CONDITIONING: a form of learning in which a neutral "conditioned" stimulus develops the power to elicit a reflexive or involuntary response as a result of repeated pairing with an "unconditioned" stimulus which naturally elicits this response.

Via classical conditioning, Colbey has learned to flinch and close his eyes when he observes someone about to slam a door. The sudden loud noise of a slamming door is an *unconditioned stimulus* which will naturally startle most people. Seeing a person about to slam the door is, in this case, the *conditioned stimulus.* The first time he observed someone assuming such a posture, Colbey did not flinch. But this observation was followed by the door slamming, the loud noise, and Colbey's startled response. After repeated pairings of a person first holding a door and then the sudden noise that followed, Colbey developed an association between the observation and the startle response. He thus became classically conditioned: the sight of someone holding a door would make him flinch in anticipation of the loud noise which had often followed that observation.

EXTINCTION: the elimination of a learned instrumental response by repeatedly not reinforcing it when it occurs; or the elimination of a classically conditioned response by repeatedly presenting the conditioned stimulus without the unconditioned stimulus.

If there were nothing intrinsically rewarding about quiet play activities, and if Colbey's mother stopped reinforcing him with treats

26

for such play, it is likely that the responses of playing quietly would gradually extinguish and that Colbey would soon revert to noisy, destructive play. He would still have the capacity for quiet play, but it would be considerably less likely to occur because recent experience has taught Colbey that it no longer led to rewards. The presence or absence of reinforcements promotes the increase, maintenance, or extinction of instrumental responses, and together they lead the individual to behave so as to maximize payoffs in particular situations. As an example of extinction of a classically conditioned response, if Colbey were startled whenever he saw someone holding a door, but if the people never slammed the doors, it is likely that the frequency or magnitude of startle would gradually decrease until the observation no longer elicited any startle response. He would still flinch if he suddenly heard a door slam, but the learned association between observing a person holding a door and anticipating a sudden loud noise would have been reduced or extinguished.

REINFORCEMENT CONTINGENCIES: the specific conditions under which reinforcements may be given for particular responses in particular situations.

A reinforcement contingency specifies the probable relationship between instrumental responses and their reinforcing consequences. For example, receiving a lollipop and praise from his mother was contingent upon Colbey playing in a quiet and appropriate way when his mother was present. The reinforcement contingency might not exist in other situations; for example, in the house without his mother around or in the playground even with his mother around.

SCHEDULE OF REINFORCEMENT: the program which dictates the occasions on which a response will or will not be reinforced.

A reinforcement contingency does not specify how often the appropriate responses will be reinforced. For example, Colbey's mother may have praised him and given him a candy after every five minutes of quiet play or after he completed a play activity, depending on the schedule of reinforcement. The schedule may change over time; at first, she might have rewarded him often, but once the behavior became well established, rewarding him on an infrequent random basis may have been sufficient to maintain the behavior. A schedule of reinforcement may be based upon response time or number of responses and may be constant or variable. Different schedules have different effects.

GENERALIZATION: the tendency to perform a response in a new situation because of the situation's similarity to the one in which the response was learned, the tendency being proportional to the degree of similarity.

If a response has been learned in one situation because of its favorable consequences, it is likely to be tried out in similar situations. For example, Colbey might generalize his behavior of playing quietly to other situations similar to his home—his friend's house or the playground. The same thing would be true of a classically conditioned response, such as Colbey's startle response when he sees someone holding a door. If the response had been conditioned in relation to his father's continually slamming the front door, and then he observed his father holding a different door, the conditioned startle response would probably generalize to this new situation. The magnitude of the generalized response would depend upon the degree of similarity between the original and the new situation.

DISCRIMINATION: learning to respond differently to each of two or more similar but distinct stimulus situations because of the different consequences associated with each one.

In some cases, a generalized response will meet the same consequences in the new situation as in the original situation, and will therefore appropriately persist in the new situation. In other cases, the new situation will be different and the response will extinguish in that situation while continuing in the original one. The person will learn to discriminate among these similar but distinct situations and behave in the different ways which are appropriate to each one. For example, Colbey generalized his response of "playing quietly" to his friend's house and to the playground. At his friend's house, the friend's mother praised him and gave him some ice cream, thereby reinforcing the behavior. As we would expect, Colbey continued to play appropriately when he was at his friend's house. In contrast, when he played quietly in the playground nobody gave him any candy, and he tended to be overlooked or ignored by his boisterous playmates. Colbey soon learned to discriminate between home and playground and rapidly returned to his rambunctious ways in the playground. Discrimination may also be learned in relation to stimuli eliciting a classically conditioned response. Although Colbey initially flinched whenever he observed his father holding any door, the only door father ever slammed was the front door because it had a defective latch. Gradually, as Colbey developed discrimination, the only scene that would evoke his conditioned startled response was seeing his father holding the front door.

PUNISHMENT: the presentation of an unpleasant or aversive stimulus in order to suppress particular behavior.

Just as a behavior will become more likely if it leads to favorable consequences (instrumental conditioning), so it will become less likely if it has no functional consequences (extinction) or if it leads to unpleasant consequences (punishment). For example, when Colbey was found writing on the wall with his crayons, his mother punished him by spanking him. This immediately suppressed the behavior and reduced the likelihood of Colbey repeating it in the future, at least when his mother was around.

29

> ESCAPE: the performance of a response in order to terminate
> aversive stimulation.

When a person experiences unpleasant stimulation, he is likely
to try to escape from the situation or the noxious stimulation associated with it. When Colbey was at the airport, he held his hands to
his ears to escape from the noise of loud jet engines. When he was
throwing a tantrum at home, Colbey's parents held their hands to
their ears. When Colbey was being spanked for writing on the wall,
he started to whimper, said he would not do it again, and looked
ashamed. His mother, touched by Colbey's overtures of guilt and
apology, stopped spanking him and let him go. Colbey had exhibited
responses which were successful in enabling him to escape from that
unpleasant situation.

> AVOIDANCE: the performance of a response in order to pre-
> vent aversive stimulation.

When a person anticipates unpleasant stimulation, he is likely
to try to avoid the situation or the expected noxious stimulation. If
Colbey put his hands on his ears as soon as he saw a plane in the
distance but before he heard it, he would avoid the unpleasant noise
of the aircraft. As another example, the next time Colbey wrote on
the wall in his room, he knew he would be punished if his mother
discovered it when she returned so he cleverly moved a large map
taped onto a nearby wall to cover up his writing. This response might
have enabled him to avoid the punishment he anticipated. However,
his mother, being comparably clever as well as suspicious, soon discovered the reason for the map's relocation. Another avoidance attempt by Colbey, blaming the artwork on his friend, was also
unsuccessful at fooling his mother, who was an experienced lie detec-
tor. All attempts at avoidance having failed, poor Colbey had to rely
on his repertoire of escape responses in order to minimize the impact
of the forthcoming punishment.

SECTION 2

Methods of Behavior
Modification

CHAPTER 4

Operant
Conditioning and
Extinction

Human behavior is largely controlled by its consequences. For example, we go places that make us feel good—shows and sports events—and try to avoid places that make us feel bad—cemeteries and rush-hour freeways. We associate with people who are nice to us and avoid those who are not. We participate in competitive activities in which we are successful, and not those in which we have little skill. We speed on the highway, but as soon as we spot an officer we slow down. We go to restaurants where the food is usually good and avoid restaurants where we have had poor meals. The basic idea is that people do what pays off for them and do not do what does not pay off. This is true of students, teachers, children, parents, princes, paupers, pets, and politicians.

Operant conditioning and *extinction* refer to a system of techniques for modifying instrumental behavior by controlling its consequences. Responses are likely to increase in occurrence if they are followed by rewards (conditioning) and to decrease in occurrence if they are consistently unrewarded (extinction) or punished. In addition to changing the probabilities of behavior patterns which already exist in a person's repertoire, operant conditioning may also be used to develop new behaviors.

Initial responses may be occasioned by special *prompts* which are then *faded* after the responses have been reinforced and increased in frequency. For example, a mother's demonstrations and verbal instructions may serve as prompts for a child's initial efforts at tucking in the cover on his bed, but gradually the amount of demonstration and instruction will be decreased (faded) as the behavior becomes reliable. New or more refined responses may be *shaped* by rewarding responses which come progressively closer to the desired ones—that is, by reinforcing successive approximations to the desired behavior. For example, the mother may initially praise the child for a sloppy attempt at tucking in the cover, but her subsequent approval will be contingent upon gradual improvement in the quality of his performance.

Responses can also be linked sequentially to form a more complex behavioral performance through a procedure called *chaining*. Here, reinforcement is first made contingent upon the last response in the chain, and then, working backwards, each preceding response is progressively made a requirement for continuation to the next link in the chain, and the preceding link becomes the stimulus for the next link. For example, bed-making behavior, which actually consists of a sequence of chained responses, would probably be trained most efficiently if Mother first taught the child the final response in the chain, namely, how to tuck in the cover (after she had already spread it out and centered it). Working backwards in the chain, she would then teach him how to center the cover prior to tucking it (after she had already spread it out), and, finally, she would teach him how to spread it prior to centering and tucking it. Training each of these component responses might require independent prompting and then shaping until an acceptable level of performance is achieved.

Environmental contingencies of reinforcement are forever shaping, maintaining, and extinguishing our behavior, often without our awareness. Behavior modification often attempts to control systematically the reinforcement contingencies so they shape and maintain adaptive behavior and extinguish maladaptive behavior. In this chapter we are concerned with the underlying principles of operant

34

conditioning and extinction and the contexts in which these procedures are central to the treatment approach.

In formulating a strategy for modifying particular instrumental behaviors, one must consider more than just the nature of the behavior, and the reinforcement contingencies which determine its consequences. Behavior does not take place in a vacuum; some environment or stimulus situation always sets the occasion for the behavior. Furthermore, a particular response may be quite appropriate in one situation and inappropriate in another. For example, a child's loud yelling might be quite appropriate in the playground or at the ballpark, inappropriate in the classroom or restaurant, and unlikely to occur while watching television or painting a picture. The environmental contingencies vary in these situations, as does the adaptiveness or maladaptiveness of the behavior. If a therapist were asked to formulate a strategy to modify the maladaptive behavior, he would not be interested in extinguishing all yelling behavior, but only in reducing the probability of its occurrence in those situations in which it is undesirable. He would thus attempt to teach the child to make finer discriminations between the playground and the classroom by permitting yelling to be rewarded in the playground but assuring that it is not rewarded (is extinguished) in the classroom.

Three factors—the stimulus situation, the behavior, and the reinforcement contingencies—must be considered in planning a treatment strategy to modify instrumental behavior. The goal is to increase the probability of the desired behavior pattern in the appropriate situation by selectively rewarding the desired response, or approximations thereto, and consistently not rewarding undesired behavior. Note that extinction does not make a response disappear from a person's repertoire but merely makes its emission less probable; in other words, it lowers the response in the person's *response hierarchy*, while other responses may be elevated in probability of emission within the hierarchy. Since extinction, alone, of a response is a long process, it is most effectively undertaken in combination with conditioning of more desirable responses which are incompatible with the undesired one in the particular situation. Specification of effective operant learning conditions and reinforcement contingencies has been much facilitated by the work of Skinner and his associates (Skinner, 1953, 1969; Ferster and Skinner, 1957).

35

In planning an operant treatment, it is often helpful to proceed in a systematic way which includes a sequence of six basic steps:

1. *Stating the General Problem.* The first step is to arrive at a general but thorough statement of the problem and description of its setting.

2. *Identifying the Behavioral Objectives.* The next step is to identify more specifically the target behaviors and the treatment goals for each of them. Behavioral objectives should include a precise description of the behavior, the conditions under which the behavior should or should not occur, and the acceptable level of the behavior's performance. Most problems will have several discrete behavioral objectives.

3. *Developing the Behavioral Measures and Taking Baselines.* In order to define the behavior at the outset and then determine how well treatment progresses, it is important to devise some way to measure the behavior—that is, to count or record the occurrence of the target behaviors associated with the behavioral objectives. These target behaviors should then be measured before any treatment is introduced in order to determine their baseline rates.

4. *Making Natural Observations.* Before one can effectively plan to change behaviors by changing reinforcement contingencies, one must first have some idea of what the existing contingencies are; that is, what contingencies currently appear responsible for controlling the target behaviors? Such an analysis will provide clues as to what constitute effective rewards for the subject and what changes in contingencies need to be made.

5. *Formulating and Introducing Modification Methods.* The next step is to decide how to alter the contingencies of reinforcement in order to fulfill each of the behavioral objectives. Arrangements must be made to reward behaviors to be increased in occurrence in particular situations and not reward behaviors to be decreased. It is therefore necessary to specify the conditions under which reinforce-

ments are or are not to be given, what the reinforcements shall be, and who shall administer them.

6. *Monitoring the Results.* Once the treatment is initiated, it is important to determine its effect. Periodically measuring and remeasuring the target behaviors and comparing the results to the baseline measures (perhaps by using a chart or graph) will indicate whether the target behaviors are changing in the desired directions. If not, reanalysis of the situation and perhaps changes in the treatment strategy may be necessary. If treatment proceeds according to plan, the periodic measurements will show when the acceptable level of performance for each target behavior, as defined under the behavioral objectives, has been achieved.

Reliable measures are essential if one is conducting an experiment to evaluate the effects of specific variables. In natural settings, however, it is often difficult to gain sufficient control over the situation to permit precise recording of behavioral measures. In such cases, the treatment program's formulation should follow the same guidelines but it may be necessary to rely upon observers' reports and subjective impressions to monitor progress. The general approach is illustrated in the following two adapted examples based on behavioral programs which were introduced in a school setting (Sherman and Sherman, 1967).

The first case involved the treatment of a youngster who inappropriately called out answers in class:

> Glen was a seven and one-half year-old boy who was repeating the first grade. His class consisted of 24 boys and girls from a middle-class New England community. His teacher was a young, competent woman who maintained a warm, controlled atmosphere in her classroom, and was well-liked by the children. According to the teacher, Glen was of average intelligence, good-looking, well-coordinated, and generally liked by his peers. The teacher reported that her main problem with Glen was that he frequently called out answers and disrupted the class. He did not raise his hand, and regardless of whether he knew the answer, he often yelled out a response from his seat in the back of the room. This tended to disrupt the class, and his classmates ordinarily turned to look at him. The teacher generally said something like, "Raise your hand, Glen, don't call out," and proceeded to call on

37

another student. This difficulty with Glen had continued for several months before the teacher sought assistance in resolving the problem.

There appeared to be two basic behavioral objectives, namely (1) Glen will not call out answers in class when the teacher asks a question, and (2) Glen will raise his hand and wait to be called on when he wishes to answer a question. Although it was not feasible in this classroom situation to arrange for precise measurements of the relevant behaviors—for example, the frequency of Glen's calling out, raising his hand, the accuracy of his answers, or the frequency of the teacher's questions —it was evident from initial observations that Glen inappropriately called out a great deal and that this behavior represented a continual disruption for the class. Analysis of the existing situation highlighted the fact that when Glen did call out an answer, this was generally followed by attention from his classmates and a comment, albeit critical, from the teacher. It therefore appeared that Glen's calling out behavior was being maintained by the social attention he received, suggesting that the contingencies be rearranged to provide social reinforcement when he raised his hand and waited to be called upon, but not when he called out.

The teacher was advised to move Glen from his seat in the back of the room to a seat in the front and center opposite her. In this way, if he called out, he would not readily observe the reactions of his classmates, reducing one major source of reinforcement, and he would also tend to call out in a lower tone since he would be nearer the teacher, thus being less disruptive. The teacher was also instructed to completely ignore Glen whenever he called out, and to praise the students who were raising their hands (which is a good idea, anyway). This would make it clearer to Glen what he could do to get positive attention under these circumstances. Furthermore, at the beginning when Glen did not call out for several successive questions, she was to praise him. Likewise, when he raised his hand, she was to praise him and call on him frequently, particularly at the beginning. Finally, when he was called on and provided a reasonably correct answer, she was to commend him further in a way that would draw the class' attention to his achievement. Thus, the basic approach was to eliminate the reinforcing social attention for calling-out behavior and instead make it contingent upon raising-hand behavior.

Within a very short time, the frequency of Glen's calling-out behavior decreased, and he began to raise his hand instead. The teacher's overtures of praise for appropriate behavior provided Glen with even more attention than he had formerly received through his misbehavior, and now it was all favorable. Glen also appeared to be tuning in more to the content of the lessons so that he could arrive at correct answers to the teacher's questions. Glen's improvements, which soon reached the point where he was no longer regarded as a problem by the teacher, were maintained for the remainder of the school year.

38

The second case involved the treatment of disorderly group behavior in the cafeteria of Glen's school:

The lunch period consisted of a half hour in the cafeteria with three first-grade and two second-grade classes, totalling about 100 children and two teachers on duty. The children were often very noisy and wild, shouting, running around, and leaving and reentering the cafeteria. Furthermore, the tables, chairs, and floor were generally left quite messy, which created a problem for the classes which followed them. Also, the teachers, who had to give up part of their lunch hour to be on duty on a rotation basis, wanted to have only one teacher on duty at a time rather than two. The principal, who was distressed about the noise which carried all the way to her office, thought that perhaps more, not fewer teachers should be on lunch duty.

There appeared to be at least five basic behavioral objectives for this cafeteria situation: (1) noise will be limited to normal conversation; (2) children will leave their seats only to return food trays, dispose of garbage, or use the restrooms; (3) each child will clean up his table and sitting area; (4) departure from the cafeteria will be orderly and quiet, without any returning; and (5) one teacher on duty will be sufficient. Initial observations revealed quite dramatically that the quality of the lunchroom with regard to noise, inappropriate activity, and messiness generally ranged from moderate disorder to utter chaos. It appeared that the children tended to reinforce each other for running around, making noise, throwing food, and so on by prompting, encouraging, and/or enthusiastically participating in the activities. Teachers tended to pay special attention to misbehaving youngsters by calling their names, scolding them, and telling them what not to do. It was also noted that the occasional appropriate and desirable behavior exhibited by the children tended to be overlooked or ignored. These observations suggested that the existing contingencies were such as to reinforce misbehavior and discourage desirable behavior; they therefore required extensive change.

In order to introduce some positive incentives for desirable behavior and to reduce the reinforcements associated with disorderly behavior, a class competition program was devised. The classes were told that they would be judged each day by the (now one) teacher on duty on the basis of behavior and cleanliness, and they were informed of the specific criteria related to such things as noise, remaining in seats, cleaning up, and leaving the cafeteria (which was now to be done on a class basis). After the classes returned to their rooms from the playground after lunch, a monitor would go around to each class and announce the one which had been best that day. The victorious class would have a star inserted on a class competition chart posted in the cafeteria, and would also have a plaque to hang on their door for the

39

day. The class with the most stars at the end of each month was to receive a special prize from the principal—ice cream, cookies, or some other treat. In addition to the reinforcement contingencies associated with the class competition, the teachers were instructed to ignore bad behavior and socially reinforce good behavior on a class basis by praising the classes which were appropriately quiet, well-behaved, and clean.

In general, right from the start, there was a dramatic improvement in the cafeteria situation. The children enthusiastically got caught up in the spirit of the competition, and individuals within a class tended to use disapproval to bring their misbehaving classmates into line. Thus the reactions of the children, which previously had been an influential force in maintaining misbehavior, now represented a powerful force in encouraging and maintaining desirable behavior. Occasionally there were mild returns of misbehavior, particularly on rainy days when the students could not go out to the playground and by classes that were far behind toward the end of a month's competition. There were also some differences in the effectiveness of individual teachers in praising desirable behavior and ignoring misbehavior. Nevertheless, the overall improvements in the cafeteria situation were considerable, which made things much more pleasant for the staff and introduced some excitement for the youngsters, who were now channeling their energies in constructive directions. The program was easily maintained with only one teacher on duty, and the improvements persisted for the remaining three months of the school year.

Several general points should be considered in formulating an operant treatment approach. First, it is important to be systematic and consistent in carrying out the program of reinforcement contingencies. The subject(s) will most readily learn the new rules of the game, which require desirable behaviors to maximize favorable payoffs, when the rules are systematically and consistently applied. For example, in the illustration above, if the teachers had varied in their standards of desirable versus undesirable behavior in the cafeteria, the children would have become confused as to what was expected of them. Initially, the children's behavior would probably have varied considerably as the teachers and their standards changed from day to day. Eventually, the children might have learned to discriminate the standards of individual teachers; they would have behaved differently depending upon which teacher was on duty. This, of course, would be an inefficient way of programming contingencies to fulfill the original behavioral objectives; it would be far more effective for all of the staff to agree on the explicit formulation of the program and cooperate in its administration.

It is often desirable to promote generalization of conditioned behavior to other settings. Although new behavior patterns are likely to show some initial transfer to other similar situations, they are unlikely to persist in the new situations unless the existing contingencies are consistent with those of the training situation (or unless the new behavior patterns become reinforcing in their own right—as in the learning of skills instrumental in the new situations, such as reading). For example, even though many youngsters learned to behave appropriately at mealtime in the school cafeteria, they would not necessarily behave more appropriately at dinner at home. If the parents praised them for good table manners, stable transfer would be likely. On the other hand, if the parents continued to scold them for making noise, leaving their seats, or being sloppy and continued to take good behavior for granted by ignoring it, the children would probably continue to misbehave at home. They would learn to discriminate the prevailing contingencies which exist in the two settings and to elicit social attention by being controlled and considerate in the school cafeteria and disruptive at home.

When feasible, reinforcements should immediately follow the performance of the desired behavior so the subject is certain just what behavior is being rewarded. Sometimes it is possible to bridge the gap between a response and a later reward by introducing a symbolic reward or explaining the reason for the reward when it is finally given.

At first, each instance of the desired behavior should be reinforced. Eventually as the behavior increases in frequency, it becomes appropriate to reward it progressively less frequently but often enough to maintain it. Such an intermittent schedule of reinforcement will increase the strength of the response and make it more resistant to extinction. For example, if a person received candy every time he put a dime into a candy machine, and then suddenly he began to lose his dimes, it would not take him long to conclude that the machine was broken. On the other hand, if the machine had always been unpredictable, paying off sometimes and not other times, one might sacrifice quite a few coins before finally realizing that something was different. It is the intermittent reinforcement associated with betting on horse races, dice, and roulette wheels that keeps the gambler hooked, even though in the long run the house usually wins.

When a behavior pattern is being extinguished by nonreinforcement, the behavior occasionally gets worse before it gets better. For example, if a boy has learned that he can get his mother's attention by teasing his kid sister, and then his mother begins to ignore him when he does this (which is introducing the extinction contingency), he will probably try even harder by poking and punching his sister before he finally gives up and seeks other ways to get his mother's attention. This will be a problem, since the danger to his sister will prompt the boy's mother to forget the plan and intervene when he begins to punch her. The boy will consequently learn that merely teasing his sister is no longer sufficient and he must now resort to punching her in order to get Mother's attention, which is quite the opposite of Mother's original objective. The moral of the story is that, before one introduces the use of extinction as the main technique to eliminate undesirable behavior, he must be sure he can tolerate the transition period in which the behavior may initially get worse before it extinguishes. This is one reason why it is wise, if possible, to combine the extinction contingency with the reinforcement of other, more desirable behaviors which are incompatible with the undesired one. At times, it may also be appropriate to use punishment to suppress the undesired instrumental behavior in order to allow more desired behavior to occur and be reinforced. This and other methods involving the use of aversive contingencies are considered in Chapter 10.

Operant conditioning and extinction procedures have been systematically used to modify a wide variety of behaviors including psychotic behaviors in adults, autistic behaviors in children, psychopathic behaviors in delinquents, and undesirable behaviors in school children as illustrated in the earlier examples. Sherman and Baer (1969) and Krasner (1971) have comprehensively reviewed recent developments in the application and evaluation of operant procedures. One of the most important innovations has been the introduction of *token economy* systems (see Ayllon and Azrin, 1968) in such settings as residential psychiatric wards and institutions for mentally retarded children. A token economy incorporates a wide range of behaviors into a system of reinforcement contingencies in which tokens—such as poker chips which are exchangeable for a variety of material goods and privileges—are used as reinforcers in much the same way money is used outside the treatment setting. Thus, while the individuals earn tokens, they also acquire desirable behaviors and skills (like washing themselves, putting clothes away, coming to meals on time, making their beds, following rules, and having good manners) which will enable them to adapt better to their social environments. Although the basic principles are the same as those used in treating individuals to achieve a single target behavior, what makes the token economy unique is the number of people and wide variety of behaviors subsumed by its program of reinforcement contingencies.

Operant conditioning and extinction procedures may often be used in conjunction with other treatment processes. The following case, adapted from Lazarus (1960), illustrates the treatment of a child's fear of moving vehicles through the operant reinforcement of adaptive approach behavior as well as the deconditioning of anxiety facilitated by feeding responses (a procedure described further in Chapter 7):

The patient, eight years old, had developed a fear of moving vehicles two years after he and his parents had been involved in an auto accident. The child refused to enter any vehicle. On one occasion when he had been unwisely forced into a car by his father, the patient became panic-stricken and hysterical.

Therapy consisted initially of talking to the patient about airplanes, buses, and trains, but even this mild exposure to the stimulus theme tended to evoke anxiety. However, whenever he volunteered a positive comment, the child was casually offered his favorite chocolate. By the third interview he spoke readily and at length about all types of moving vehicles, there no longer being any evidence of overt anxiety.

The next stage of treatment consisted of presenting a series of deliberate accidents with toy motor cars, and a fairly high level of anxiety was initially exhibited. After each accident the patient was given chocolate, and subsequently his anxiety dissipated and he entered into the full spirit of the game. The child was next seated in a stationary motor car and was provided with liberal helpings of chocolate throughout a discussion regarding the accident in which he had been involved. Thereafter the child was taken in a car for short distances.

43

Less than six weeks after therapy had commenced, at the seventeenth session, the patient willingly entered a car and, accompanied by a complete stranger, they set off for a shop where he bought chocolate. At first, the child refused to go motoring with his parents unless he was given chocolate, but he soon began to enjoy motoring for pleasure [p. 116].[1]

As a final illustration of the extensive control which can be exerted over instrumental behaviors by manipulating the contingencies of reinforcement, we will summarize a case presented by Haughton and Ayllon (1965) in which the response of broom-holding was intentionally shaped and then extinguished in a psychotic patient:

The subject was a 54-year-old schizophrenic who had been hospitalized for 23 years. According to ward reports she stayed in bed or lay on a couch most of the time and was an idle patient who refused to do anything in the ward except smoke. To develop in the repertory of the patient a novel class of behavior which was selected to be holding a broom while in an upright position, cigarettes were used as a reinforcement. A period of response shaping was initiated during which a staff person gave the patient a broom; while she held it, another staff member approached the patient and gave her a cigarette. Intermittent reinforcement was then used to condition the behavior.

In a few days, the patient developed a stereotyped behavior of pacing while holding the broom. Eventually, it was possible to maintain the behavior through the use of conditioned reinforcers which were tokens exchangeable for cigarettes. During the final phase of the experiment, extinction was introduced to insure the elimination of broom-holding behavior. All reinforcement for broom-holding was withdrawn, and eventually the behavior of carrying the broom was no longer displayed by the patient. According to the authors, in a two-year follow-up there was no record of the response ever recurring [pp. 96–97].[2]

[1]Adapted from Lazarus, A. A., "The elimination of children's phobias by deconditioning." In Eysenck, H. J. (Ed.), *Behaviour Therapy and the Neuroses.* Copyright 1960 by Pergamon Press. This and all other adaptations from the same source are used by permission.

[2]Adapted from Haughton, E., and Ayllon, T., "Production and elimination of symptomatic behavior." In L. P. Ullmann and L. Krasner (Eds.), *Case Studies in Behavior Modification.* Copyright 1965 by Holt, Rinehart & Winston. Used by permission.

This experiment was primarily intended to demonstrate that stereotyped and repetitive behaviors, often exhibited by psychotic people, may be developed and controlled through environmental contingencies.

Issues to Consider

1. In deciding how to implement an operant treatment program, one is often faced with the question of whether to explain to the subject exactly what is to take place. We know that a person's behavior may be controlled with or without his awareness. In the cases presented in this chapter, we observed varying degrees of initial awareness. Glen was not told that the teacher was going to try a new strategy to eliminate his calling out, and he may not have been aware (at least initially) of the changes taking place in the situation and in him. What do you think would have happened if the new contingencies had been explained in advance to Glen? Would this have accelerated or interfered with the behavior changes?

The children in the cafeteria were told very clearly what the new rules of the game were and what behavior they had to exhibit to succeed in the class competition. What do you think would have happened if they had not been given an advance explanation, but were left to discover the rules themselves?

In the example of conditioning and extinction of broom-holding behavior, the woman was not told that she would receive cigarettes for holding the broom. Do you think she would have been able to verbalize an explanation of the contingencies if she had been asked later in the experiment?

If she had been a negativistic person who generally resisted staff interventions and was told in advance about the experiment, do you think this would have caused her to avoid the broom intentionally just to frustrate the staff's efforts because frustrating the staff was more rewarding for her than smoking?

In some instances it might be clear whether advance explanations would accelerate or jeopardize a treatment program, and in others it might not be so clear. Can you formulate basic guidelines

45

concerning when and when not to include explanations in the introduction of an operant treatment program?

2. If an operant treatment program is to be successful, rewards
must in fact be reinforcing for the subject. An adult is unlikely to
perform well for candies, and a two-year-old child is unlikely to
perform well for dollar bills. How can the therapist determine in
advance what are effective incentives for the subject population?

Some effective rewards might be identified by observing the
behavior of the subjects in natural settings, by talking with people
who are familiar with them, or by asking them directly. Primary
reinforcers such as food, water, and sleep will probably motivate
people who have been deprived of them. The relative effectiveness
of secondary reinforcers—such as material goods, privileges, coins,
and social approval—may be more variable and difficult to predict;
for example, the priest may be more motivated by social concerns
than by the acquisition of wealth, whereas the thief uses under-
handed means to acquire wealth and is unconcerned with social
approval. Similarly, candy and toys may work well in motivating
performance in mentally-retarded youngsters who do not respond to
social reinforcers, whereas the cheers of fans may be more important
in sustaining the performance of high school athletes than any concern about material rewards. Can you think of any basic differences
between your own motivational hierarchy and that of some close
friends?

Educators believe that the student's incentive for attending
school is to acquire knowledge and understanding. Many students
report that their main incentives include the social life, earning degrees, and the promise of better jobs; they say that most studying is
for grades and not necessarily knowledge. How could the traditional
structure of educational institutions be modified to reduce these
inconsistencies and make the educational experience more pleasant
and profitable?

This is certainly a very important and challenging problem
which warrants much more attention than it has received.

3. Manipulating reinforcement contingencies to condition desirable behavior patterns would not be particularly useful if it were

necessary to continue them forever in order to maintain the behavior. Instead, what should happen if the behavior is in fact adaptive is that it will meet with favorable environmental consequences directly associated with the nature of the behavior itself. For example, an operant program using candy as a reward may be used to teach a youngster to play with other children or to teach a mentally-retarded person to comb his hair. Once the behavior is established, the new satisfactions derived from social play or from looking neat should be sufficient to maintain it. Certainly we all perform numerous behaviors which do not appear to be dependent upon the immediate delivery of extrinsic rewards. Can you think of any responses or skills which you learned under the incentive of some special reward, but which have persisted for other reasons?

Perhaps summer jobs you took on in order to earn money also taught you some skills—gardening, preparing sandwiches, or carpentry—which continued to be useful for their own sake. Can you think of any behaviors which were no longer useful to you and were abandoned after the original incentives were withdrawn?

4. The notion that behavior is extensively influenced through environmental reinforcement contingencies and that we are all continuously being controlled in this way may be disputed by those who believe that man's free will controls his behavior. The question of determinism versus free will has always been a central philosophical issue. Psychology, with its focus on the prediction and control of behavior, is basically deterministic in orientation. Skinner's *Walden Two* (1948) is a utopian novel which illustrates the possible use of positive reinforcement contingencies to control virtually all behavior within a society, purportedly to maximize the good for everyone. Proponents of this objective maintain that, since our behavior is being controlled anyway, contingencies should be arranged so as to promote the most desirable behaviors (from the standpoint of the preservation of the culture) while providing the greatest rewards for its individual members. This position is further elaborated in Skinner's *Beyond Freedom and Dignity* (1971).

Some critics maintain that such a controlled society is not possible because man's behavior is more than a response to reinforcement contingencies. Other critics maintain that such a society would not be desirable because it would reduce the behavioral variability among people, would discourage creativity, and would retard the progress of mankind. Do you think such a controlled society, in which man's basic needs are readily fulfilled and frustrations are minimized, would be a desirable thing?

Do you think it is theoretically possible?

If so, do you think it is a practical possibility, and what would you wish to have included?

If a utopian society based upon reinforcement principles were possible, do you think it should be designed by psychologists, sociologists, philosophers, ministers, or political leaders? In fact, can you think of anyone whom you would trust to design and administer such a society?

Small communities based upon Skinner's *Walden Two* are being attempted.[3]

---

[3]In a personal correspondence, Skinner informed me that a community modeled on *Walden Two*, called Twin Oaks, is located at Route 4, Box 169, Louisa, Virginia 23093. Twin Oaks has been in existence since 1967. Members publish a newsletter concerning their activities and progress and also have information about other experimental communities.

CHAPTER 5

Systematic Desensitization

Systematic desensitization is a method of treatment designed to help a person overcome fear reactions to specific objects or situations. Such stimulus-specific fears are often called *phobias* to distinguish them from generalized or pervasive anxiety which does not appear to be related to any special circumstances. Another characteristic of phobias is their irrationality. Certain fears would be regarded as realistic—for example, fear of poisonous snakes or fear of being injured in military combat—whereas phobias are irrational in that the fears are unrealistic or out of proportion to actual circumstances.

It is usually presumed that one develops a phobic reaction as a result of some adverse or traumatic experience with similar or related situations. The similarity may be along physical dimensions—for example, a painful bee sting may lead to a fear of all small flying insects; or it may involve symbolic mediation—for example, strict discipline by a punitive father may lead to a fear of all authority figures. According to the principle of *primary stimulus generaliza-*

tion, it is not only the original stimulus which will evoke a conditioned fear reaction; stimuli similar to it along some dimension will evoke the fear reaction as well. The greater the similarity to the maximum phobic stimulus, the stronger the evoked fear; the less the similarity, the weaker the fear.

Phobic reactions may develop in relation to many objects or situations, but some phobias are more common than others and even have their own names. These include fear of heights (acrophobia), darkness (nyctophobia), open places (agoraphobia), animals (zoophobia), closed spaces (claustrophobia), dirt or germs (mysophobia), and crowds (ochlophobia). Generally, the degree of fear experienced by the person is directly related to quantitative aspects of the feared situations: for example, the closer one is to the feared situation, the more afraid he is. Phobias are therefore maladaptive because they unnecessarily cause the person to avoid harmless situations or to experience severe distress if exposure is unavoidable. Before considering systematic desensitization as a possible treatment for a phobic reaction, the behavior therapist would first make sure that the feared situations were objectively harmless and presented no demands which the client lacked the skill to handle.

Systematic desensitization therapy is based on a person's inability to be both relaxed and anxious at the same time; the autonomic effects which accompany deep relaxation—decreased pulse rate, blood pressure, and skin conductivity and slower and more regular respiration—are opposite to the autonomic effects which characterize anxiety. According to Wolpe (1962), who developed the systematic desensitization treatment, "If a response inhibitory to anxiety can be made to occur in the presence of anxiety-evoking stimuli, it will weaken the connection between these stimuli and the anxiety responses [p. 562]." In accordance with this *reciprocal inhibition* principle, systematic desensitization attempts to substitute muscular relaxation for the tension response of anxiety which represents the person's present reaction to the phobic stimuli.

Therapy begins with *predesensitization,* which includes training in relaxation and composing an anxiety hierarchy. The client is initially trained in the technique of *progressive deep relaxation* by a procedure based on the work of Jacobson (1938). By alternately tensing and relaxing specific muscle groups, he learns to discriminate

50

feelings of tension and relaxation in his muscles, and to relax them more and more deeply. He is also instructed to practice the relaxation procedures at home. Auxiliary techniques such as imagining oneself in relaxing situations or concentrating on breathing may be used to further deepen relaxation. Eventually, the well-trained client should be able to relax his entire body deeply in a few minutes.

Concurrent with relaxation training, the therapist attempts to explore the history and current status of the phobic reaction. The theme of stimuli occasioning the reaction—for example, heights, deep water, or animals—would already have been identified since the therapist has decided to use systematic desensitization. Now the client is asked to describe a wide variety of situations related to the phobic theme and to rate subjectively the intensity of the distress aroused by each one. The client may use a rating scale, for example, going from 0 (comfortable and relaxed) to 100 (extremely tense and anxious) to rate his reaction to the phobic situations. The situations are then ranked from the least to the most threatening to form what is known as an *anxiety hierarchy*. This ordinarily consists of a list of about 20 to 25 items related to the phobic theme which span the entire range of distress. For example, the person who is afraid of heights might identify "standing on a one-foot stool," "climbing up a six-foot ladder," and "looking down from the balcony of a twelfth-story penthouse," as being low, middle, and high items on the hierarchy.

It is generally considered important for the anxiety hierarchy to be thoroughly representative of the phobic theme without any large gaps in the anxiety ratings between adjacent items. Using our hypothetical 0-to-100 anxiety scale, the anxiety hierarchy would ideally consist of items spaced at approximately five-point intervals. Of course, as treatment progresses, changes or refinements in the anxiety hierarchy may be required.

After the relaxation has been mastered and the anxiety hierarchy formulated, the actual *desensitization* is begun. This procedure attempts to maintain the fear response at a very low magnitude by initially presenting the client with stimuli which are low on the anxiety hierarchy. The stimuli are presented by *imagery;* that is, the client is instructed to imagine himself in the stimulus situations. Relaxation responses, presumed to be incompatible with anxiety and

51

tension, are then used to inhibit the small amounts of tension which would otherwise be evoked. As long as the relaxation responses are stronger than the tension responses, the relaxation responses will predominate and counteract the tension evoked by the mildly threatening stimulus. With several repeated presentations of the stimulus, and in the absence of any adverse consequences, its tension-evoking potential will progressively decrease to zero. This *counterconditioning* of the tension response will likewise generalize to other stimuli on the anxiety hierarchy so that they, too, will lose some of their tension-evoking potential. Thus, once the weakest stimulus has ceased to arouse any tension or anxiety it will be possible to present the next higher stimulus from the hierarchy, for it will now evoke less anxiety than it would have done before. With successive presentations to the relaxed client, the amount of anxiety aroused by each imagined stimulus will be brought to zero, with further generalization to related stimulus items. A graded approach may then be used along the anxiety hierarchy, at each stage the stimulus situation being made more like the maximum phobic stimulus, with relaxation responses being used to counteract and decondition the tension responses.

In practice, the client is given several minutes to relax himself while the therapist suggests how the client may further relax. The client is then asked to imagine himself in the scene represented by the next least disturbing item in the anxiety hierarchy. The therapist describes the situation, tells the client to imagine himself in it, and then instructs him to stop imagining it after about ten or 15 seconds. If the anxiety evoked is of low intensity, as it should be if the item was properly selected, it will be counteracted by the relaxation, and the anxiety potential will progressively decrease to zero with another one or two presentations of the item. If the client finds that the image is causing excessive tension, he is instructed to signal by raising his forefinger and is then told by the therapist to stop the image. The item is then presented again, generally in a milder version or a briefer exposure. After each item is completed, the next one is presented until it ceases to evoke any anxiety on two or three successive presentations.

Eventually, after several sessions of this desensitization procedure, stimuli at the highest levels in the hierarchy may be imagined by the client without arousing any anxiety. Of course, for the treatment to be regarded as successful, the client would have to be able to be comfortable in the real phobic situations, not just the imagined ones. Just as the emotions evoked by a situation during a dream or a movie are often similar to experiencing the real situation, Wolpe (1961) maintains that eliminating anxiety to an imagined stimulus in systematic desensitization readily leads to freedom from anxiety when the real stimulus is confronted. Some research evidence challenging this hypothesis will be described later in the chapter.

In a paper on procedural factors of systematic desensitization, Lazarus (1964) elaborated on certain technical details and specific variations—the signalling of anxiety, the number of, duration of, and interval between scene presentations, and the optimal interval between sessions. Wolpe and Lazarus (1966) also devote a section to such procedural and quantitative factors. Further consideration of such methodological details would lead us away from our general survey of behavior modification treatments. However, it must be emphasized that specialized knowledge and supervised training are essential for the successful administration of this and all other therapeutic procedures.

The basic procedures of systematic desensitization are illustrated in the following case adapted from Lazarus and Rachman (1957):

> The patient was a 14-year-old boy who suffered from a four-year phobia of ambulances and hospitals. He reported that he was frightened by the sight of ambulances and avoided them however and whenever possible, to the extent of planning his journeys in advance and changing direction when an ambulance was sighted. He stated that he had fainted on several occasions when an ambulance was nearby. The patient was also afraid of hospitals and nursing homes and refused to visit them. His social and scholastic adjustments were both satisfactory.
>
> After an initial period of training in relaxation, systematic desensitization was begun. Separate hierarchies of noxious situations were constructed for the ambulance and hospital phobias. The ambulance hierarchy ranged from such nondisturbing stimuli as a parked ambulance in the distance and a derelict ambulance in a junkyard to difficult ones like sitting in the back of an ambulance. The first easy situation in the hospital hierarchy was a distant hospital which could be barely seen, and the final one was a surgical ward.

Soon after the third desensitization session, the patient walked past a parked ambulance with its rear doors open and experienced no anxiety. During the course of therapy two similar situations occurred, neither of which evoked fear reactions. After ten interviews the patient was much improved and was able to approach ambulances and visit the hospital without difficulty. No recurrence of the earlier fears were reported after a three-month period.[1]

The following case of a heat phobia, adapted from Kraft and Al-Issa (1965), is presented to further illustrate systematic desensitization therapy. It is also interesting because of its theoretical implications regarding the possible traumatic basis of specific phobic behavior and the fact that the treatment succeeded despite the patient's amnesia of the original traumatic event.

The patient, a 24-year-old female with an IQ of 120, had been suffering from heat phobia dating from the age of five. Details of her early history were initially obtained from her mother and were confirmed by the patient, under hypnosis, after the treatment had been completed. When she was five years old, the patient witnessed a fire in which the charred bodies of two children were carried out of a burning house. She was reportedly terrified by the whole event but appeared to show remarkably little emotional reaction toward it and subsequently developed complete amnesia.

The patient developed phobic symptoms in relation to heat almost immediately after the traumatic incident. She showed great reluctance to put her hands into warm water and washed herself in relatively cold water (about 72° F.) which she, however, regarded as fairly warm. As a child, she was terrified of striking a match and succeeded in doing so for the first time at the age of 14. She also found it difficult to drink and eat hot foods. Later, she found she could not touch an electric hotplate even when it was turned off, and she could not use a hot iron. At the age of ten, she first realized that she avoided looking at the burns on the left side of her aunt's face because this gave rise to anxiety. On several other occasions, looking at burns produced a great deal of anxiety. The patient had received psychiatric treatment at various hospitals, including electroconvulsive therapy and various drug combinations, but there was no alleviation of the present symptoms.

[1]From *South African Medical Journal,* 1957, **31**, 934–937. Copyright 1957 by the Medical Association of South Africa. Used by permission.

Systematic desensitization treatment seemed indicated, and relaxation was induced by hypnosis. A list of anxiety-provoking situations was compiled by the patient with the assistance of the therapist. This list consisted of items related to two modalities, visual and tactile. Temperature was the operative anxiety-provoking factor in all the stimuli presented. The items were arranged in ascending stress value from low temperature regions, where the patient was completely anxiety-free, and increasing gradually to higher temperature levels. In all, 16 stimulus situations using visual imagery only were presented to the patient. The number of hierarchies for each item depended on the nature of the stimulus situation. For example, the item "seeing water heated" was divided into 33 temperature levels, beginning at 55° F., which was completely anxiety-free, and increasing by successive 5-degree intervals to 210° F. When this temperature had been reached, a further increase of 2 degrees raised the temperature of the water to the boiling point, 212° F. Similarly, when the patient was presented with the item "putting her hands into the oven," this was divided into 68 temperature levels starting at 215° F. and increasing by 5-degree intervals to 550° F. Note that the incident which gave rise to the patient's phobia, and for which she was amnesic, was not included in the stimulus hierarchies.

After four practice hypnotic sessions, 37 desensitizing sessions of one hour's duration were carried out. During the treatment sessions, practically all items required only one presentation, and a few required two presentations. The treatment was continued for a period of two months. Early in the course of the treatment there was apparent improvement in the patient's phobic symptoms. Thus, after the eighth desensitizing session, the patient found that she could enjoy washing up in hot water, using a hot iron, and sitting in the sun. Heat became less and less distressing to her and she became enthusiastic to reach higher temperatures. As treatment progressed and particularly after the fourth desensitizing session, the patient reported a gradual change in her judgment of temperature. This increased with each session until a temperature of 73° F., which was regarded as "warm" before the treatment began, was regarded as "cold" when the treatment ended. Similarly, at the onset of her therapy she became acutely anxious when coming into contact with water at a temperature of 118° F. Following the treatment, however, she could momentarily put her fingers into water at a temperature of 140° F. without any anxiety.

Following the course of treatment, the patient became completely anxiety-free in all aspects of her heat phobia. A follow-up after 12 months showed that she remained symptom-free [pp. 55–56].[2]

[2]Adapted from *Behaviour Research and Therapy,* 1965, **3,** 55–58. Copyright 1965 by Pergamon Press. Used by permission.

The theory and effectiveness of systematic desensitization have been variously supported and challenged. Of 68 anxiety hierarchies formulated in the systematic desensitization therapy of 39 patients (some with multiple phobias), Wolpe (1961) reported that 91 percent were overcome or markedly improved in a mean of 11.2 treatment sessions per hierarchy. In addition to the successful clinical outcomes reported by Wolpe (1961), Lazarus (1963), and others, systematic desensitization has been evaluated favorably in experimental studies dealing with such fear reactions as public speaking anxiety, fear of closed spaces and heights, fear of snakes and spiders, and examination anxiety (see Paul, 1969a, 1969b). A number of reports have suggested certain theoretical and/or practical limitations of the treatment, including incomplete transfer of anxiety elimination from the imagined to the real situations (Agras, 1967; Davison, 1968; Sherman, 1969), and the relative ineffectuality of the treatment when therapeutic instructions and verbal positive reinforcement were omitted (Leitenberg, Agras, Barlow, and Oliveau, 1969).

In general, the literature on systematic desensitization can be classified under three major categories: (1) suggestions, usually based on clinical data, regarding the modification of certain aspects of the standard desensitization procedure or the introduction of new innovations within the same framework; (2) studies evaluating the characteristics and relevance of certain aspects of the procedure and/or the validity of certain theoretical principles underlying the procedure; and (3) clinical or experimental studies designed to evaluate the overall effectiveness of the procedure, sometimes in comparison with other treatment procedures. Two such studies follow.

A comprehensive experiment on the relative effectiveness of systematic desensitization was conducted by Paul (1966) working with 96 college student volunteers who were afraid of speaking in public and who were enrolled in a required course on public speaking. Five psychotherapists worked individually with one female and two male students in each of three treatment procedures for five hours over a six-week period. The three treatment conditions included systematic desensitization therapy, insight-oriented psychotherapy consisting of the conventional procedures used by the therapists in their traditional practices, and an attention-placebo treatment incorporating the nonspecific factors of relationship, attention, suggestion, and expectation of relief. In addition to the 45 students in the three treatment conditions, 29 students were in a no-treatment control condition and 22 students were in a no-contact control condition.

On the basis of a variety of measures of public speaking anxiety which were obtained before and after the treatment period, systematic desensitization was found to be the most effective treatment, with 86 percent of the students showing much improvement and the remaining 14 percent showing some improvement. No difference was found between the effects of insight-oriented psychotherapy (20 percent much improved and 27 percent improved) and the attention-placebo treatment (47 percent improved), although both of these groups showed greater anxiety reduction than the no-treatment controls (17 percent improved). A short-term follow-up revealed that improvement was maintained by those who had received the systematic desensitization treatment. There was no evidence of symptom substitution, and a two-year follow up (Paul, 1967) further confirmed the durability of the improvements.

Several reports (Agras, 1967, working with multi-phobic patients, and Davison, 1968, working with snake-phobic students) have suggested that eliminating anxiety from imagined situations by systematic desensitization does not necessarily transfer completely to the real situations. In the study by Paul (1966) described above, which reported virtually 100 percent success in only five treatment sessions, all subjects were concurrently enrolled in a required public speaking course which included classroom speeches. In contrast, the lesser efficiency and effectiveness of systematic desensitization in a study by Lang, Lazovik, and Reynolds (1965) treating snake-phobic students may have been due to the absence of concurrent experience with snakes. In this study, ten of the 23 subjects who received systematic desensitization completed fewer than 15 out of 20 anxiety hierarchy items and showed little improvement after 16 treatment sessions.

In view of these considerations, I speculated that the effectiveness of systematic desensitization in bringing about real-life reduction in fear may depend to some extent upon client exposure to the real situations during the course of the treatment. In other words, it was hypothesized that if systematic desensitization were conducted in imagery while the client also had some exposure to the real situations in his daily life, there would be greater improvement than if there were no such real exposure.

To test some of these ideas, a study was conducted (Sherman, 1969, 1970, 1972) with 54 female college students who had irrational fears related to swimming or being in the water. Each aquaphobic student received one of six treatment conditions which were administered on an individual basis by six psychologists and five psychological assistants. One of the basic treatment procedures, consisting of gradual exposure to the real phobic situations, will be discussed in Chapter 7. Our present concern is primarily with the two treatment conditions which consisted of systematic desensitization with versus without real-life exposure. The systematic desensitization procedure consisted of seven 50-minute sessions, and the real-life exposure involved three sessions of about 15 minutes each.

The results showed that although students who received systematic desensitization without exposure succeeded in imagining the situations from their anxiety hierarchies without any anxiety, this desensitization of anxiety to the imagined stimuli showed little transfer to the real-life situations. These students and their therapists initially thought that they were less afraid at the end of the treatment, but when the students were placed in the real-life situation of a swimming pool, they exhibited almost as much fear and avoidance behavior as they had before the treatment. In contrast, students who received systematic desensitization with exposure generally exhibited much real-life improvement as well as subjective feelings of improvement. These findings led to the conclusion that real-life exposure may facilitate the desensitization treatment of certain phobic reactions. Further research is needed to clarify this issue and others concerning the theory and practice of systematic desensitization.

Issues to Consider

1. The theory and method of systematic desensitization require that the client begin by imagining the mildest items in the anxiety hierarchy and gradually work up to the most threatening items. Do

you think that the graded aspect of the approach is necessary, and why?

As you will discover in Chapter Six's discussion of implosive therapy, some behavior therapists believe it is more effective to begin right at the top by confronting the client with the situations that evoke the greatest fear in him. What are your initial thoughts about this idea?

2. According to the theory of systematic desensitization, relaxation plays an important role in the treatment because it purportedly functions to counteract the anxiety evoked by images of feared situations. What do you think would happen if the treatment were conducted without relaxation training, that is, if the client were asked to visualize himself in the series of graded situations without instructions to relax?

The basic theoretical question here is whether the behavior change taking place during systematic desensitization is a result of so-called reciprocal inhibition (or counterconditioning), based on the contiguity of muscular relaxation with anxiety stimulus visualization, or a function of extinction, based only on the repeated visualization of the anxiety stimuli without any adverse consequences. This important issue has represented the focus of several investigations and debates (Davison, 1968, 1969; Folkins, Lawson, Opton, Jr., and Lazarus, 1968; Folkins, Evans, Opton, Jr., and Lazarus, 1969) but has still not been entirely resolved.

3. The systematic desensitization treatment appears to depend on how realistically the client can imagine himself in the situations he fears. The treatment rationale assumes that the client can turn on an image of a situation, experience it as though he were really there, hold it for several seconds, and then turn it off again. How valid do you think this assumption is?

See how well you can control your own fantasies by closing your eyes and imagining that you are in an office on the eighth floor of a building in the city; you walk over to the window, open it, stick your head out, and look down at the noisy traffic and the people in the street below you.

The person who is afraid of heights would probably be terrified by the prospect of carrying out this activity. However, the effectiveness of systematic desensitization would theoretically depend on how realistically he could imagine himself in such situations. Do you think relaxation might play a role in facilitating the visualization of feared activities which phobic persons would ordinarily avoid?

4. Children often fearfully avoid situations or objects which are not threatening to adults. As most children get older, such phobias ordinarily tend to disappear. Perhaps examining some of the factors that account for this tendency will enable us to improve treatment procedures for those who retain their phobic reactions. Contributory factors toward reducing fears in daily life are: (1) the child becomes more physically and intellectually skillful and better able to cope with his environment; (2) he often appears to rehearse the feared situations in his fantasies and dreams and acts them out in play; (3) he observes his playmates exhibit no distress in the feared situations; and (4) he occasionally becomes exposed to the feared situations and nothing bad happens as a consequence. In thinking about some of your own childhood fears, which of these factors (or any others) do you think were most important in accounting for their resolution?

What implications do you think this analysis might have for the formal treatment of fear reactions, and for systematic desensitization in particular?

5. The medical model emphasis on identifying and resolving underlying causes has prompted some psychodynamically-oriented therapists to challenge the behaviorists with the prediction that other symptoms will arise if a behavioral treatment changes only overt behaviors without dealing with the presumed underlying causes. The absence of any such apparent symptom substitution is then sometimes used by behaviorally-oriented therapists to counterattack the theory of psychodynamic causes. What is your opinion of these arguments?

One difficulty in assessing the processes involved in changing behavior through imaginal desensitization methods is that there is no reliable way to know what the person is imagining. Suppose the visualizations at times actually include situations or events related to causal factors. For example, a psychodynamic analysis of a person with phobic reactions toward large dogs might suggest that the phobia represents a manifestation of an underlying conflict related to ambivalent feelings toward a punitive father, which are then displaced onto symbolically related objects, in this case, large dogs. Perhaps in systematic desensitization when the person is instructed to visualize himself entering a room with a large dog present, he also has flash images of being in a room with father. A psychodynamic theorist might even predict that being in a deeply relaxed state would facilitate the recovery of such unconscious memories because the forces which maintain the repression would be reduced. Thus, even though imaginal desensitization treatments are not directly concerned with such possibilities, it might be that the psychodynamic causes become desensitized in the process, as well. On the other hand, this notion might have no validity at all. What is your opinion?

How would you go about formulating a research study to investigate this issue?

CHAPTER 6

Variants of Imaginal Desensitization

Since the introduction of systematic desensitization, several variations of that treatment have been developed which also rely upon the client imagining feared situations to bring about a reduction in phobic anxieties. These variations include group treatment of clients with a common phobic problem, the use of procedures other than relaxation training to evoke responses intended to counteract the anxiety responses, and the nongraded presentation of maximally threatening imaginal situations for prolonged periods to promote a direct extinction of the evoked fear. We will discuss these variants next.

Group Desensitization

In group desensitization, clients with a common phobic reaction are treated in a group setting by procedures which differ only slightly from those employed in individual systematic desensitization. Thus, the clients are trained in deep muscular relaxation, and a group anxiety hierachy, incorporating all of the relevant anxiety-evoking situations expressed by individual clients, is constructed. As in individual treatment, the desensitization sessions follow the pattern of having the clients relax and then presenting them with successive items from the anxiety hierachy for visualization. The procedure is conducted at the pace of the most anxious person; that is, an upward step is taken in the hierarchy only when every client has been able to complete the previous item without anxiety. Although this is likely to increase the number of sessions required for the completion of treatment for the group, it may still prove considerably more efficient for the therapist because fewer sessions are spent per client.

The effectiveness of group desensitization has been demonstrated by Lazarus (1961) in the treatment of several different phobic problems, and by Paul and Shannon (1966) in the treatment of public speaking anxiety. Lazarus, in an attempt to compare the effects of group desensitization with that of a more traditional form of psychodynamic group psychotherapy, worked with a total of 35 middle-class urban whites with a mean age of 33.2 years. The sample included 11 acrophobics, 15 claustrophobics, 5 impotent men treated as suffering from sexual phobia, and a mixed group of 4 phobic subjects. The subjects were matched and then randomly assigned to small treatment groups of from two to five; with one exception, the clients in each group shared a common phobic reaction. All treatments were conducted by the experimenter. Of the 18 subjects treated by group desensitization, 13 (72 percent) were free of phobic symptoms after a mean of 20.4 sessions, although three relapsed as of a nine-month follow-up. With the dynamically-oriented interpretive treatment, only two subjects out of 17 (12 percent) were found symptom-free after a mean of 22 sessions, both of these having attended groups in which relaxation was employed as an adjunct to the interpretive procedures. Of the 15 subjects who derived little benefit from the psychodynamic group therapy, ten became symptom-free in a mean of only 10.1 sessions when subsequently treated by group desensitization. The relatively short time required for desensitization in these patients was presumed attributable to the therapeutic relationship and other nonspecific factors inherent in the prior psychodynamic therapy.

63

In the Paul and Shannon (1966) study, ten male college students were treated for public speaking anxiety in two desensitization groups of five subjects each, treatment being limited to nine sessions conducted on a weekly basis. These subjects had previously completed a speech course at the time they were evaluated as untreated controls in an earlier investigation (Paul, 1966; see p. 56 of this book) comparing the effects of individual systematic desensitization, insight-oriented psychotherapy, and attention-placebo treatment. The results revealed a significant reduction in maladaptive anxiety and improved college grade-point average following the group desensitization. The combined group desensitization treatment was superior to both the individual insight-oriented and attention-placebo treatments of the earlier investigation with comparable subjects, and on a par with the individual systematic desensitization treatment. It was concluded that "the method of systematic desensitization previously found effective in individual treatment can be efficiently combined with group discussion and administered in groups without loss of effectiveness in the treatment of interpersonal performance anxiety [pp. 132–133]."

Directed Muscular Activity

Training in relaxation is central to systematic desensitization. However, some people are unable to learn how to relax themselves deeply enough. For such clients, *muscular activation* may sometimes be used instead of muscular relaxation to counteract the anxiety responses associated with the imagined situations (Lazarus, 1965).

As in standard systematic desensitization, an anxiety hierarchy is formulated and the client is requested to visualize himself in the situations of the hierarchy, beginning with the mildest items. However, instead of relaxing, as soon as he has formed a vivid image of the scene, he is instructed to engage in vigorous muscular activity such as hitting a punching bag or slamming his hands and arms on a pillow. Lazarus (1965) claimed that "almost invariably, this vigorous motor expression seems to produce a temporary obliteration of the ongoing scene and its subsequent return at a slightly weaker level of anxiety or disturbance [p. 302]." The procedure is continued until the imagined scene no longer evokes any subjective distress; it is repeated for the remaining items working from the least to the most threatening.

The following case, adapted from Lazarus (1965), briefly illustrates the fundamentals of using directed muscular activity in imaginal desensitization:

> The patient, a 32-year-old male with a debilitating fear of visiting dentists, was treated by desensitization. Relaxation and hypnotic procedures were abandoned because he became acutely upset by a heightened awareness of his own heartbeat whenever these measures were applied. He was then desensitized by means of directed muscular activity wherein he vigorously pounded a leather-padded footstool during the visualization of hierarchy scenes. His hierarchy consisted of 22 items ranging from the word "dentist," to the phrase "the dentist pushes the needle into your gums." After 16 consecutive daily sessions, the patient visited a dentist for the first time in six years and underwent two extractions and five fillings with normal trepidation.[1]

Although it appears inconsistent that two apparent opposites, muscular relaxation and muscular activity, can both have anxiety-inhibiting effects, there is some evidence that motor responses may have an inhibitory effect upon autonomic responses (Wolpe, 1958, p. 173). The method is fairly new, and additional research is required to determine its therapeutic effectiveness and to clarify the underlying mechanisms.

Emotive Imagery

Self-relaxation and the ability to turn discrete images on and off are skills which require a high degree of concentration to learn and carry out. Because of their shorter attention spans and verbal ineptitude, many children would have difficulty following the instructions and mastering the skills required for systematic desensitization therapy. Lazarus and Abramovitz (1962) have developed a related method for treating phobic reactions in children which circumvents

---

[1]Adapted from *Behaviour Research and Therapy*, 1965, **2**, 301–304. Copyright 1965 by Pergamon Press. Used by permission.

some of these problems. Their method, called *emotive imagery*, makes use of personal images which arouse positive feelings of strength, affection, pride, excitement, or adventure. These images are then incorporated into a story and the resulting positive emotional responses counteract the anxiety associated with phobic scenes gradually introduced within the story.

As with systematic desensitization, early in treatment the therapist and client formulate an anxiety hierarchy. However, instead of training him in self-relaxation, the therapist talks with the child about the things he would like to do or would like to be. In this way, the therapist attempts to identify the nature of the child's fantasies, wishes, hero images, and the feelings which accompany them. The child is then asked to close his eyes and imagine a sequence of events close enough to his everyday life to be personally meaningful, but within which is woven a story involving his positive wishes or fantasies. Then, when it appears that the positive emotions have been aroused in the child, the lowest item in the anxiety hierarchy is introduced as a natural part of the narrative. The positive emotional feelings are expected to counteract the mild anxiety associated with the hierarchy item in much the same way the relaxation responses are presumed to counteract the anxiety in systematic desensitization. The method proceeds as in systematic desensitization with progression through the hierarchy as each item is incorporated into the imagined story without distress.

The following case illustration of the use of emotive imagery is adapted from Lazarus and Abramovitz (1962):

> The patient, a 14-year-old-boy, suffered from an intense fear of dogs which had lasted for two and one-half to three years. He would take two buses on a roundabout route to school rather than risk exposure to dogs on a direct 300-yard walk. He was rather a dull (IQ = 93), sluggish person, very large for his age, trying to be cooperative, but sadly unresponsive—especially to attempts at training in relaxation. In his desire to please, he would state that he had been perfectly relaxed even though he had betrayed himself by his intense fidgetiness. Training in relaxation was eventually abandoned, and an attempt was made to establish the nature of his aspirations and goals. By dint of much questioning and after following many false trails because of his inarticulateness, a topic was eventually tracked down that was absorbing enough to form the subject of his fantasies, namely, racing motor-cars.

He had a burning ambition to own a certain Alfa Romeo sports car and race it at the Indianapolis 500. Emotive imagery was induced as follows: "Close your eyes. I want you to imagine, clearly and vividly, that your wish has come true. The Alfa Romeo is now in your possession. It is your car. It is standing in the street outside your house. You are looking at it now. Notice the beautiful, sleek lines. You decide to go for a drive with some friends of yours. You sit down at the wheel, and you feel a thrill of pride as you realize that you own this magnificent machine. You start up and listen to the wonderful roar of the exhaust. You let the clutch in and the car streaks off. You are out in a clear open road now; the car is performing like a pedigree; the speedometer is climbing into the nineties; you have a wonderful feeling of being in perfect control; you look at trees whizzing by and you see a little dog standing next to one of them—if you feel any anxiety, just raise your finger. . . ." An item fairly high up on the hierarchy was: "You stop at a café in a little town, and dozens of people crowd around to look enviously at this magnificent car and its lucky owner; you swell with pride; and at this moment a large boxer comes up and sniffs at your heels. If you feel any anxiety. . . ."

After three sessions with this method, the patient reported a marked improvement in his reaction to dogs. He was given a few field assignments during the next two sessions, after which therapy was terminated. Twelve months later, reports received from both the patient and his relatives indicated that there was no longer any trace of his former phobia.[2]

As with many other novel therapeutic methods, the data on emotive imagery is primarily of a clinical nature. However, the favorable clinical findings should prompt investigators to conduct controlled experiments to evaluate this promising approach further.

Imaginal Desensitization with Drugs

Another way to pursue desensitization is to use tranquilizing drugs to promote or facilitate deep relaxation. The client may be instructed to take a prescribed tranquilizer before each desensitization session; he would then be likely to arrive somewhat more re-

[2]Adapted from *Journal of Mental Science*, 1962, **108**, 191–195. Copyright 1962 by The Royal College of Psychiatrists. Used by permission.

laxed, and it might also be easier for him to relax further using the standard relaxation procedure.

A more elaborate use of drugs as an adjunct to imaginal desensitization involves intravenous injection of a tranquilizing drug during the office treatment session. The short-acting barbiturate methohexitone sodium, also known as Brevital, has been used for this purpose. In addition to reducing the need for preliminary training in deep muscular relaxation, injecting the tranquilizer directly into the bloodstream permits increased control over the timing and depth of the induced relaxation.

There have been several clinical reports on the effectiveness of imaginal desensitization with drug-induced relaxation. For example, Friedman (1966) reported that 25 cases of phobic anxiety which he treated by this method all responded well and were symptom-free at the end of treatment, which required a mean of 12 sessions. Brady (1966) reported marked improvement in four out of five cases of chronic frigidity, a condition in which intense anxiety is often the factor which interferes with satisfactory sexual performance. Brevital was used to induce deep relaxation in order to facilitate the imaginal desensitization of the clients' sexual anxieties. The mean number of sessions required was 11.

On the negative side, Reed (1966) has commented on a number of difficulties he encountered in using Brevital in desensitization therapy. He indicated that some patients dislike receiving the intravenous injections, some find the initial induction period unpleasant, and with some it is difficult to control the depth or duration of the induced relaxation. The consensus of several recent reports on this treatment method is more favorable, suggesting that some of the technical difficulties may have been overcome.

Implosive Therapy

Systematic desensitization is characterized by a brief and graded presentation of the imaginal phobic stimuli. According to the theory, the client must never experience any distress, or at least not enough to exceed the strength of the relaxation responses. Therefore, treatment begins with brief visualizations of the mildest items

68

in the anxiety hierarchy, and presentation of the higher items occurs only after their fear-evoking potential has been sufficiently decreased as a result of generalization of extinction from the lower items.

Although the theoretical rationale is clear, it is appropriate to question whether the systematic, gradual presentation of feared stimuli for brief intervals is the most efficient and effective way to proceed. What would happen if the client were required to imagine himself in the most threatening situations for prolonged periods right from the start, without any relaxation responses, in order to bring about a very strong fear response? Perhaps such a frightening experience would ultimately lead to a more rapid extinction of the fear rather than making the client more afraid. This view prompted Stampfl's development of a method called *implosive therapy*, which has the client visualize himself in the situations he finds most disturbing (Stampfl and Levis, 1967).

In implosive therapy, the therapist describes each situation vividly; he includes details about the worst possible consequences of the experience, attempting to evoke a maximal level of anxiety in the client. It is assumed that the anxiety will eventually begin to dissipate as a result of the sustained visualization. As the client appears to show some reduction in his anxiety response to the imagined scene, the therapist introduces new variations in order to elicit again a maximally intense anxiety response. The treatment continues in this manner, and the client is also instructed to practice imagining the scenes between treatment sessions. When the anxiety associated with all of the highly threatening scenes is extinguished, the therapist generally introduces new scenes related to the problem which he suspects may be even more threatening to the client, but which the client may not have been able to identify. For example, a person who is suffering from guilt feelings and a fear of punishment might be instructed to visualize himself as the recipient of intense anger, hostility, and physical aggression as a result of engaging in specific forbidden acts. Eventually, it is presumed that all of the anxiety associated with the phobic theme or hypersensitivity will extinguish and the client will be cured.

According to Stampfl and Levis (1967), "the fundamental hypothesis is that a sufficient condition for the extinction of anxiety is to re-present, reinstate, or symbolically reproduce the stimuli (cues) to which the anxiety response has been conditioned, in the absence of primary reinforcement. . . . The more accurate the hypothesized cues and the more realistically they are presented, the greater the extinction effect would be [pp. 498–499]." The effectiveness of the treatment would therefore appear to depend on the skill of the therapist in identifying the relevant anxiety-evoking cues and presenting them in dramatic detail for the client to imagine.

Stampfl and Levis (1967) maintain that implosive therapy is quite efficient in promoting behavioral improvements, with the total treatment time rarely exceeding 30 one-hour sessions. They report from clinical experience that implosive therapy "appears to be highly effective over a wide range of psychoneurotic disorders including anxiety, phobic, obsessive-compulsive, and depressive reactions and has been applied successfully to psychotic disorders including affective, schizophrenic, and paranoid reactions [p. 502]." Several experimental studies (Kirchner and Hogan, 1966; Hogan and Kirchner, 1967, 1968; Wolpin and Raines, 1966) have also found implosive therapy to be effective in treating individuals who fear rats or snakes. On the other hand, Wolpe (1969, p. 192) described one of several clinical cases in his experience who appear to have gotten worse as a result of flooding procedures similar to implosive therapy, and experiments by Rachman (1966) with spider phobias and Mealiea (1967) with snake phobias were also not favorable to the implosive method. It would appear that further research is needed to determine the circumstances under which implosive therapy might and might not be appropriate.

Issues to Consider

1. Group desensitization may represent a positive innovation because it enables a therapist to simultaneously treat several clients who have the same phobia. From the practical standpoint, however, a particular fear reaction is unlikely to be so common and troublesome as to be presented by several people seeking treatment at the same time. One possibility is to treat different phobias in a heterogeneous group by having clients progress according to the

item numbers of the scenes in their personal anxiety hierarchies, rather than having the therapist describe each scene as he would in a homogeneous group with a common hierarchy. Can you envision any problems with such a method, or do you think it would succeed?

Some fear reactions such as public speaking anxiety, fear of taking examinations, and fear of various social situations are common, but people do not generally seek private treatment for them. For such problems it might be desirable to offer group treatment through public agencies, perhaps as self-improvement courses through adult education programs. If such a group desensitization program for one of your own fear reactions were conveniently available at little or no cost, would you voluntarily participate?

2. Directed muscular activity to counteract anxiety does not appear theoretically consistent with the use of muscular relaxation for the same purpose. Let us try an experiment. If you were asked to describe three experiences or situations that you, personally, find relaxing, what would you name?

You may have included some passive situations like lying down at the beach or listening to soft music, but you may also have included some active experiences like playing golf, bicycling, or dancing. Many people find such activities to be subjectively relaxing. Certainly, the person who is playing tennis would not be muscularly relaxed in the same way as if he were reclining in an easy chair practicing the self-relaxation method. However, he might regard himself as psychologically relaxed in the sense that he is not thinking about his various worries—perhaps his job or his family. The anxiety-inhibiting effect of both muscular relaxation and muscular activation in therapy may result from focusing one's attention on his body and away from his various worries. As long as the person has nothing on his mind which causes him distress, he is likely to be subjectively comfortable and relaxed. If you think this possible explanation has any validity, how could it be studied experimentally?

3. Emotive imagery can deeply involve children in stories since play activities and fantasies are very real to youngsters. However, there is a puzzling aspect of the mechanisms presumed to underlie

the emotive imagery method: why is it that the youngster, when he encounters the feared situation in reality, does not discriminate between the unrealistic fantasies he was instructed to imagine in therapy and the real-life situation in which he is alone without his Alfa Romeo or the help of his best friend, Superman?

Has he learned to imagine that these supports are with him when he encounters the feared objects in real life? If so, this would seem to create more problems than it resolves. Instead, it seems the child is expected to discriminate between the imagined and the real events with respect to the fantasied supports, but not with respect to the phobic features (Sherman, 1971). This aspect of the child's cognitive experience in emotive imagery therapy would appear to be quite complex and worthy of further study.

4. Imaginal desensitization with drug-induced relaxation would appear to increase the efficiency of treatment and circumvent some of the problems associated with people who have difficulty relaxing themselves. However, the relationship between self-induced relaxation and drug-induced relaxation is not clear. In the first case, the client has his bodily state under his own control; to a large extent, he is able to turn the relaxation on and off at will. In the case of drug-induced relaxation, control is exercised primarily by the effects of medication upon the body's nervous system. Perhaps the bodily changes resulting from self-induced and drug-induced relaxation are in some ways different. If research were to be conducted on this question, what criteria might be used to decide which of the two relaxation-induction methods would be preferable as an anxiety-inhibitor?

A related issue is to what does the client attribute his progress, and does this have any effect upon the transfer and stability of his improvement? One view might maintain that the improvement resulting from imaginal desensitization with self-induced relaxation would show more transfer because the person could attribute his progress largely to his own relaxation skill; consequently, he would feel more in control of his tensions and less vulnerable to stressful situations than if his progress were attributed to a drug which is absent when he encounters the feared situations in reality (see Davison and Valins, 1969). An alternative view might maintain that the improvement resulting from imaginal desensitization with drugs would show more transfer and stability because of the person's confidence in drugs, as generated from prior experiences of relief when receiving drugs for physical illnesses. Which method would give you more confidence in the permanence of your improvement if you had undergone imaginal desensitization?

5. Implosive therapy is meant to maximize the intensity of anxiety through highly threatening, sustained visualizations, whereas systematic desensitization attempts to minimize the anxiety evoked by mildly threatening, brief visualizations. Although the two approaches appear to have opposing methodologies, both claim to have been derived from learning theory and both provide evidence of clinical success. On the basis of your understanding of principles of learning, which of the two approaches do you believe has a more valid theoretical rationale?

If you had a phobic reaction, which type of treatment would you prefer?

CHAPTER 7

Real-Life
Desensitization

The desensitization methods presented in Chapters 5 and 6 all require the client to imagine himself in the situations he fears. Probably the main reason for using imagery is that it is generally easier for the therapist to ask the client to visualize himself in situations than it would be to present him with the real situations. Of course, the effectiveness of the imaginal desensitization methods depends on the extent to which the imagined situations are experienced as comparable to the real ones. Not all individuals are able to imagine themselves realistically in anxiety-generating situations with the appropriate affect. Even for those who can, there may be differences between imagery and reality which limit the amount of improvement that transfers from the imagined to the real situations. Some of these problems may be avoided if the therapist can arrange for the client to be exposed to the real situations.

Although real exposure may not be feasible for certain phobic fears, in many instances the necessary conditions can be arranged. Such *real-life desensitization* may involve (1) presenting the client with the feared stimulus objects (such as insects, animals, or knives) in the office; (2) showing the client photographs or films of the objects or situations, which is a compromise between imaginal and real-life desensitization; (3) the therapist accompanying the client outside the office, perhaps traveling in a car, entering a swimming pool, or riding in an elevator; or (4) arranging for the client to expose himself systematically to the real situations in his daily life. These methods may include attempts to evoke specific responses, such as relaxation, to counteract the anxiety directly or they may rely entirely upon the extinction effects of exposure without adverse consequences. Several such methods of real-life desensitization follow.

Real-Life Desensitization with Relaxation Responses

One method of real-life desensitization is to present the client with actual items from his anxiety hierarchy while he is relaxed. First, the client relaxes himself deeply, and then the therapist gradually presents the feared objects. Beginning with objects at the mild end of the anxiety hierarchy, the therapist initially presents each item at a distance and gradually brings it closer to the client until, eventually, the client can touch and handle it without distress. If the phobia is a fear of certain situations, such as being in high places, crowds, or enclosed spaces, it may be possible to instruct the client to relax himself before entering each of the situations represented in the anxiety hierarchy. This can be done whether the client carries out the systematic exposures by himself or is accompanied by the therapist.

Cooke (1966) performed a study in which one of the treatment conditions consisted of real-life desensitization with relaxation. The subjects who received this approach were four female college students who were afraid of laboratory rats. The treatment consisted of four therapy sessions at three-day intervals in which performance of the task described by a hierarchy item was alternated with periods of relaxation. Each item was repeated until the subject reported no anxiety and the therapist observed no signs of anxiety. This method of treatment led to a decrease on each of three measures of specific fear.

Real-Life Desensitization with Feeding Responses

As mentioned previously, it is often difficult to teach children to relax themselves systematically. However, responses associated with eating have been found to counteract anxiety; because feeding responses are relatively easy to evoke in hungry youngsters, they have occasionally been used in conjunction with the real-life desensitization procedure. As early as 1924, Mary Cover Jones described the method she employed successfully in the treatment of children's fear reactions:

> During a period of craving for food, the child is placed in a highchair and given something to eat. The fear-object is brought in, starting a negative response. It is then moved away gradually until it is at a sufficient distance not to interfere with the child's eating. The relative strength of the fear impulse and the hunger impulse may be gauged by the distance to which it is necessary to remove the fear-object. While the child is eating, the object is slowly brought nearer to the table, then placed upon the table, and finally as the tolerance increases it is brought close enough to be touched. Since we could not interfere with the regular schedule of meals, we chose the time of the mid-morning lunch for the experiment. This usually assured some degree of interest in the food and corresponding success in our treatment [p. 388].

The following illustration of a case treated by Jones was adapted from a description by Watson (1930):

> Peter was an active and eager child approximately three years old, who was well adjusted to ordinary life situations but feared rabbits, white rats, fur coats, feathers, cotton wool, frogs, fish, and mechanical toys. Eventually the procedure of direct unconditioning was employed.
>
> We did not have control over his meals, but we secured permission to give him his mid-afternoon snack, consisting of crackers and a glass of milk. We seated him in a highchair at a small table, the room being about 40 feet long. Just as he began to eat his lunch, a rabbit was

76

displayed in a wire cage of wide mesh. We displayed it on the first day just far enough away not to disturb his eating. This point was then marked. The next day the rabbit was brought closer and closer until disturbance was first barely noticed, and this place was then marked. The third and succeeding days followed the same routine. Finally the rabbit could be placed on the table and then in Peter's lap. Next, tolerance changed to positive reaction. Finally he would eat with one hand and play with the rabbit with the other. . . .

After breaking down his fear reactions to the rabbit—the animal having previously evoked fear responses of the most exaggerated kind —we were next interested in seeing what his reactions would be to other furry animals and furry objects. His reaction to white rats was found to be greatly improved, and fear responses to cotton, the fur coat, and feathers were entirely gone: he would look at them, handle them, and then turn to other things [pp. 172–174].[1]

Real-Life Desensitization
with Sexual Responses

A variety of sexual disturbances in males and females are psychological in origin, and inadequate sexual responsiveness or performance is often caused by the presence of anxiety. A basic objective in treating anxiety-based sexual disturbances is to reduce the anxiety and tension elicited by the sexual situation. Since sexual arousal and anxiety are to some extent incompatible, one way to proceed is to control the situation so that the strength of the sexual arousal exceeds the strength of the anxiety throughout the desensitization process. When anxiety produces a complete inhibition of sexual responsiveness, imaginal desensitization may initially be helpful to reduce the anxiety to a point where at least some sexual arousal may be exhibited.

Having established some sexual responsiveness in the client, sexual arousal may then be used systematically to counteract the residual anxiety associated with the sexual situation and related activities. Given the prearranged cooperation of a sexual partner, the

[1]Adapted from J. B. Watson, *Behaviorism.* Copyright 1924, 1925 by The People's Institute Publishing Company, Inc. Copyright 1930 by W. W. Norton & Company, Inc. Copyright renewed 1952, 1953, 1958 by John B. Watson. Used by permission.

basic strategy is for the client to approach the partner and engage in activities only so far as pleasurable feelings of attraction and sexual arousal predominate. As long as the sexual arousal is maintained at a stronger level than the anxiety, some reduction of the anxiety potential is likely on each occasion. The reduction in anxiety may then permit further advances in sexual arousal and activity which, in turn, are likely to promote further reductions in anxiety. For sexually naive or inexperienced clients, instruction in sexual techniques may be required and is available in the form of many popular books on the subject. Eventually, after a series of real-life desensitization experiences with technical instruction where required, anxiety should extinguish and adequate sexual performance should emerge.

As an example, if the anxiety was found to focus upon sexual intercourse, the client would be advised merely to lie next to his partner in a relaxed way at the beginning and to proceed no further than mild caressing on the next few occasions. It would be emphasized that he should never attempt more than he can do without complete freedom from anxiety. Eventually, increasingly close approaches to coitus are likely to become possible: after successful superficial contact, varying degrees of insertion and finally increasing amounts of movement may be attempted.

The following case treated by Lazarus (adapted from Wolpe and Lazarus, 1966) illustrates the therapeutic use of sexual responses in the treatment of sexual disorders:

> Mrs. W., aged 24, who had been married for one and one-half years, complained that she had never obtained sexual satisfaction and that in the past year she had invariably experienced such violent pain during intercourse that coitus had become insufferable. She was both grateful for and troubled by the fact that her husband had made no sexual advances for the past five months. She felt that things couldn't go on like this, but was filled with trepidation at the idea of resuming sexual relations. Further discussion revealed that her husband suffered from premature ejaculation. Mrs. W. was nevertheless convinced that her inability to obtain sexual satisfaction was entirely her own fault. She had grown more tense and upset with each successive sexual failure until the eventual impasse.
>
> Her husband, a 28-year-old engineer, was interviewed, and he acknowledged his tendency to ejaculate almost immediately upon intromission. His sexual ineptitude had caused him to denigrate himself at

78

all levels, although he was in fact adequate at his work and in social relationships.

At a joint interview, the therapist instructed the couple to resume love-making, but to proceed no further than kissing and caressing. A week later they were advised to extend the range of physical activities but never to proceed beyond the point where both remained entirely at ease and free from anxiety. They were informed that the act of coitus should not be attempted until both had attained manually induced orgasms. In his wife's presence, Mr. W. was told how to induce an orgasm by manual stimulation of the vulva, vagina, and clitoris.

Their pattern of love-play during the next two and one-half weeks was confined to heavy petting while in the nude, Mr. W. obtaining sexual relief through manual stimulation by his wife. Mrs. W. was, however, at this stage averse to manual stimulation as a means of achieving orgasm. They were therefore instructed to wait until Mrs. W. felt fully ready. This transpired within a month, and soon both were enjoying orgasm through manual stimulation.

The following love-making sequence was then proposed: they would kiss and caress as usual and Mrs. W. would satisfy her husband manually. Mr. W. would then apply manual stimulation to his wife. If he became rearoused during the course of this intimacy, they would have coitus. It was impressed upon them, however, that Mrs. W. was to achieve sexual satisfaction one way or the other. Mr. W. soon discovered that he was able to delay ejaculation almost indefinitely the second time around.

Over some three to four months the couple developed a well-formulated sexual sequence. First there was mutual masturbation to the point of orgasm, which Mrs. W. came to achieve very rapidly. After a brief rest, they would resume love-play, become aroused again, and have coitus which usually culminated in orgasms for both. Attaining mutual coital satisfaction hinged on the fact that Mrs. W.'s new-found positive responses (emanating from digital orgasms) enabled them to discover that Mr. W. was able to delay ejaculation during coitus. Success made Mr. W. a more proficient lover, enhancing their mutual pleasure.

This couple has now reportedly enjoyed a full and happy sex life for over five years [pp. 110–111].[2]

Hamilton (1925) described 200 cases he treated by procedures purportedly based on an objective behavioral analysis. The following

[2]Adapted from J. Wolpe and A. A. Lazarus, *Behavior Therapy Techniques: A Guide to the Treatment of Neuroses.* Copyright 1966 by Pergamon Press. This and all other adaptations from the same source are used by permission.

delightful report of his successful treatment of an erection-sustaining difficulty is included not only to illustrate further the effective therapeutic use of sexual responses but also because of the common sense of his approach.

The client was a male in his fifth decade who complained of the disappearance of his erection at the critical moment. There were no apparent physical factors involved, and the symptoms appeared to represent conditioned fear reactions.

He was "a robust, physically sound man with a good sexual history until the present difficulty began a few months before he came under observation. He had returned home at the end of a day of unusually strenuous physical activity, mildly overstimulated with alcohol, pleased with the day's work and in good spirits. At bedtime the stimulating effects of the alcohol had faded, and he felt his fatigue. Nevertheless, the sexual relation seemed to be in order as a kind of celebration of the day's successes, in which both he and his jolly, good-natured wife were rejoicing. He recalls that he was very tired, and not much stimulated sexually; and that his erection was not a vigorous one. It faded when he was about to copulate with her, whereupon she teased him a good deal, asserting that he was 'no good,' that he had 'lost his manhood,' etc. He was accustomed to such friendly bantering, but never before had he had the least difficulty in proving his potency to her entire satisfaction. This time he 'felt a little sheepish, and worried in spite of himself,' lest the expected copulation would be impossible because his erection would not return. A few nights later, when he was about to copulate with his wife, she referred to his previous failure and banteringly suggested that he was 'no good,' whereupon he again lost his erection. This was accepted by both of them as a great joke, and ever afterward, whenever copulation was imminent, his wife would laugh and make the usual joke. He soon found that always at the critical moment he was overtaken by a lively fear that his erection might fade and, of course, it did fade. The whole situation seemed to him to be ridiculous, but he would go to bed with strong sexual feelings and a vigorous erection, only to experience the now habitually recurring fear of a failing erection, with disastrous consequences.

"He was given some tincture of nux vomica [a stimulant] and told to refrain from attempts at copulation for three weeks. On his return at the end of this period he reported, to my disappointment, that he had been obedient to my orders. Another period of rigid continence was prescribed, but before the time was up he returned, reporting that he had successfully 'broken over' and inquiring, rather anxiously, if his disobedience would interfere with his cure. He was told that the cure was contained in the disobedience, and the principle of the conditioned reaction was explained to him. He was of the jovial, competent, 'extraversive' type for whom demonstration had best precede explanation [pp. 124–125]."[3]

The treatment success in this case might be at least partially explained by reciprocal inhibition, wherein the sexual drive was increased to predominate over the encumbering fear. Note, however, that although the impotence appeared to originate with the man's drinking and fatigue on one occasion, it was maintained by other factors such as his attention to nonsexual stimuli—his wife's taunting comments and his fear of failure. A complete understanding of the development and maintenance of the problem therefore requires attention to both respondent and operant factors.

Although this section has focused on a real-life desensitization approach to the treatment of sexual problems involving anxiety, note that other behavioral treatment procedures have also been used for this and related sexual disturbances. Some of these methods have been described in detail by Masters and Johnson (1970).

Real-Life Desensitization with Drugs

If it is considered desirable in real-life desensitization to evoke responses for directly counteracting the anxiety, and if the use of relaxation, feeding, or sexual responses is not appropriate or feasible, then tranquilizing drugs may be used. The most basic method is to administer the drug before exposing the client to the real feared situations, at a sufficiently strong dosage to assure that a fear reaction and consequent avoidance behavior will not occur. If an anxiety hierarchy is used, the dosage would probably be somewhat lower than if the client were exposed directly to the most feared situations at the outset. In either case, some evidence suggests that learning which occurs while the subject is under the influence of a drug may not readily transfer to the nondrug state.

[3]From Hamilton, G. V.: *An Introduction to Objective Psychopathology*, St. Louis, 1925, The C. V. Mosby Company. Reprinted by permission.

One possible way around the problem of *transfer decrement* associated with drug removal is to withdraw the drug gradually. *Gradual drug withdrawal* was investigated using laboratory rats with conditioned fear reactions (Sherman, 1967). The animals had learned to press a lever for food pellets; they were then punished by shock for pressing the lever. This induced an approach–avoidance conflict in which there was very little lever-pressing even after the shock contingency had been removed. The therapeutic question, then, was how to recondition the fearful hungry animals to press the lever.

During the first session of the reconditioning phase, sodium amytal, a fear-reducing sedative, was administered at a high dosage to two-thirds of the animals, who then exhibited a significantly greater number of lever presses than did the remaining saline control group which had not received the drug. In the second reconditioning session, the drug was no longer administered to half of the animals who had received it during the first session, and the performance of this sudden-withdrawal group declined to the level of the saline control group, illustrating transfer decrement. In contrast, the remaining gradual-withdrawal group received the drug at progressively reduced dosages during the second and succeeding reconditioning sessions, and they continued to exhibit further improvement in lever-pressing with no evidence of any performance decrement when the dosage finally reached zero during the fifth reconditioning session. Gradual drug withdrawal thus appeared to promote the extinction of fear and the recovery of adaptive behavior with full transfer to the nondrug state.

The following case of Rachman's, reported by Wolpe (1958), illustrates the therapeutic use of gradual drug withdrawal in a real-life desensitization framework:

The patient, a severe and intricate case of agoraphobia of five years' standing, had become worse during two years of psychoanalysis and then made considerable progress after about 18 months of hypnotic desensitization combined with graduated tasks, so that whereas at first he could not venture in space beyond the bounds of his house and his shop next door, he was now able to travel without disturbance about two miles from home by car. But progress was slow, and he was eager to return to Australia, the land of his birth. Thereupon, Rachman, in collaboration with the patient's general practitioner, embarked upon a course of treatment which was described as follows:

On January 18, half an hour after a subcutaneous injection of Pethidine (Demerol) 100 mg. [the relaxant, which was to be gradually withdrawn] and Scopolamine gr. 1/200, he went on a drive in his car in the company of his family physician. They travelled about six miles from home and remained away one and one-half hours. In the course of this time, he felt marked relaxation, dryness of his mouth, and sleepiness, but not the slightest fear despite the presence of apprehensive thoughts. The experiment was repeated on January 24, with the use this time of only 75 mg. of Pethidine, and was again completely successful. On January 27, having been given 50 mg. of Pethidine and Scopolamine gr. 1/200 (a dose which was constant for all injections), the patient took the wheel and went on a long drive with his wife and me, again feeling completely relaxed throughout. He was given several more treatments of this kind, during which the dose of Pethidine was brought down first to 50 mg. and then to 25 mg. Altogether he had nine treatments in the course of two and one-half months, and the range of his excursions progressively increased. Finally, on March 18, he left Johannesburg with his family for Durban en route to Australia. They travelled by car, and before they set out he was given a last injection containing 25 mg. of Pethidine. He arrived in Durban without mishap and without anxiety. I received a letter from him written from the ship on arrival in Australia, saying that he was feeling fine and eating enormously [p. 203].[4]

Gradual Exposure Therapy

The preceding methods of real-life desensitization included the evocation of specific responses intended to counteract the anxiety associated with the feared situations. It is often inconvenient and sometimes impossible to use relaxation or feeding responses during the real-life desensitization process, and occasionally the use of such procedures may lead to a transfer decrement. Fortunately, the extinction of fear does not require the presence of specially-evoked incompatible responses, but may be brought about entirely through repeated exposure to the feared situations in the absence of adverse consequences. In fact, exposure to the feared situations in natural circumstances is probably an important factor in the normal reduc-

[4]From J. Wolpe, *Psychotherapy by Reciprocal Inhibition.* Copyright 1958 by Stanford University Press. Reprinted by permission.

tion of common childhood fears. Provided that a situation is objectively harmless, each exposure to the situation is likely to bring about a further decrease in the evoked fear as well as generalizing extinction to related situations.

Relying upon extinction in natural circumstances tends to be inefficient because the nature of a phobic fear is such that the individual is likely to try to avoid the feared situations. Unless exposure occurs, no extinction will ensue, and with the exception of accidental confrontations, exposure in natural circumstances will probably be limited to the least threatening situations. *Gradual exposure therapy* attempts to accelerate this by systematically arranging conditions of graded exposure and repetition to bring about a reduction in fear and avoidance behavior. As with the other methods of real-life desensitization, the essence of this approach is to expose the client gradually to the real situations represented in the anxiety hierarchy, progressing along the hierarchy as each situation is successfully negotiated until the client has confronted the entire range of feared situations without distress. When this point is reached the phobia may be considered eliminated, since transfer decrement has been precluded by not using imagery or incompatible responses.

Gradual exposure therapy is not new. In a classic paper on methods of overcoming fears in children, Jersild and Holmes (1935) described the results of interviews they conducted with parents. They found the procedure of graded stimulus presentations, although not often used by parents, was reportedly very successful when it was employed. This consisted essentially of "leading the child by degrees into active contact with and participation in the situation that he fears: presenting the stimulus at first in a less intense form, or without some of its most frightening features, or in conjunction with reassuring features, and then gradually introducing all of the conditions that initially evoked fear [p. 102]." Jersild and Holmes (1935) provided several examples of how the method was used successfully:

> In dealing with a child who was afraid of the flow of water from faucets, the mother made it a policy to get him accustomed to a small flow of water, she then gradually increased the flow; to overcome a fear of alarm clocks, the parents used a clock with a softer ring, and then later

84

introduced the louder clock; the mother herself begins to cut the child's hair in the barber shop (where he previously was afraid of the general situation), while he grows accustomed to the chair and the surroundings, and then lets the barber finish the job; a child was given a smiling mask as a first step in overcoming a fear of masks that was first exhibited in response to a mask with "sinister" features; to cope with fear of the dark, a child was first given a very dim light in his room and then subsequently this light was withdrawn [p. 87].

One attempt to investigate experimentally the method of gradual exposure therapy was performed in treating aquaphobia (Sherman, 1969, 1972). As mentioned in Chapter 5, the subjects were female college students with unrealistic fears related to swimming or being in the water. The gradual exposure procedure, which was one of several methods explored in the study, consisted of presenting the student with a hierarchically arranged series of water activities in a swimming pool, with instructions to perform only those activities about which she felt comfortable. There were 26 water activities represented in the hierarchy, beginning with such mild items as "Walk over to the ladder at the shallow end of the pool" and "Climb down the ladder and stand in the water," and proceeding to such high items as "Swim underwater in the deep water for about five seconds" and "Dive in, arms and head first, off the diving board." Each student's personal level of swimming proficiency determined the range of water activities which were objectively safe for her to perform, and treatment progress was assessed behaviorally in terms of individual improvement in performing safe activities which had been fearfully avoided.

A gradual exposure procedure ordinarily lasted about 15 minutes. The eight students who received several sessions of this procedure as their only treatment showed significant improvement both in terms of behavioral performance and self-ratings of swimming anxiety. The value of the gradual exposure procedure was further revealed in relation to a required college swimming course which occurred after the treatment period. Three gradual exposure procedures had been administered as a basis for behavioral measurement to virtually all 54 students who participated in the treatment program, and 46 of them (85 percent) proceeded to pass the swimming course. In contrast, of 80 fearful nonparticipants who were comparable in swimming aptitude and slightly less aquaphobic than the participants, only 41 (51 percent) passed the course. This superior performance of the participants suggested that the improvements derived from the treatment program were durable and transferred effectively to important real-life behavior. In view of its apparent efficiency and effectiveness, gradual exposure therapy should be further studied to determine whether it might be the preferred desensitization treatment for certain fear reactions.

Issues to Consider

1. Real-life desensitization with relaxation responses is primarily intended to eliminate maladaptive fear responses to specific stimulus situations. However, as a result of the recurrent contiguity between the stimuli and the relaxation responses, the relaxation responses might be expected to become conditioned to the stimuli so that, when the individual subsequently encounters the situations, rather than being neutral towards them, he would actually become relaxed (Sherman, 1971). Using your understanding of basic principles of learning, would you make such a prediction, and why?

One question is whether an individual can become conditioned to relax deeply in response to specific cues. If so, then such training might, itself, benefit many of us since it would help us control our anxieties and cope more effectively in stressful situations. Just think how nice it would be if all you had to do to relax was ring a buzzer. Unfortunately, I am not aware of any cases in which clients treated by desensitization with relaxation subsequently reported that the situations they used to fear now relax them. Can you think of any methods that might systematically condition positive feelings in response to a signal such as a buzzer?

One possible method, called anxiety-relief conditioning, which relies upon terminating aversive stimuli to condition positive responses of relief, will be discussed in Chapter 10, "Aversion Therapy."

2. Real-life desensitization with feeding responses brings up the same question: would exposure to the previously feared situation evoke salivatory or digestive responses? Recall the case of Peter and

his fear of furry animals (p. 77): "Finally the rabbit could be placed on the table and then in Peter's lap. Next, tolerance changed to positive reaction. Finally he would eat with one hand and play with the rabbit with the other." Do you think that children such as Peter who are desensitized with feeding responses would eventually learn to salivate when they see the previously feared objects?

Although real-life desensitization with feeding responses is generally not used with adults, you have probably observed people who eat whenever they get anxious or upset. This may help control their anxiety in the short run, but do you think it has some long-term effect of desensitizing the person to the situations or experiences which originally caused the distress?

Certainly, if the only lasting consequence of eating when anxious is obesity, then this would not appear to be a particularly adaptive response to stress.

3. Real-life desensitization with sexual responses requires a cooperative sexual partner. If the client is married, this ordinarily presents no problem. However, aside from the practical difficulties of arranging suitable partners for the unattached client, some people have raised moral and ethical questions about the approach. Do you think it would be wrong to use this desensitization method with a client who, although unmarried, had a cooperative partner?

Suppose the therapist had a list of professionals who were specially trained to help people with sexual disturbances. Do you think it would be acceptable to use such a psychosexual worker in the real-life desensitization treatment?

Consider the dilemma of the person who gets extremely anxious in sexual situations. His anxieties cause him to avoid close relationships with members of the opposite sex, and as a result he never has the opportunity to overcome his apprehension and gain experience. It is a vicious cycle. If it were either practically impossible or morally objectionable to arrange for a suitable partner to assist in the desensitization treatment of such a client, can you think of any alternative procedures?

4. Real-life desensitization with drugs has the initial practical advantage that certain drugs reliably reduce anxiety and promote

relaxation. In a time of stress, one individual may take a tranquilizer prescribed by his physician; another individual may drink alcoholic beverages or smoke marijuana at social gatherings. Having discovered that these drugs relax him or make him feel good, an individual may begin taking them in other situations when he is under duress. Because they succeed in reducing his experience of anxiety, he will be reinforced and may further increase the frequency of their use. Thus, although initially used only on specific stressful or social occasions, tranquilizers, alcohol, or marijuana eventually may be taken regularly to keep users feeling comfortable or good all the time. Furthermore, because some tolerance for the drugs develops, the dosages may be progressively increased or the person may begin taking other drugs which are more potent. The reinforcement contingencies seem to be such as to lead many people into a vicious cycle of dependence on drugs which ultimately may bring about serious impairment to their psychological and physical health. What systematic methods might alter the contingencies in order to help a person out of this cycle at an early stage?

Suppose an individual went about his normal business while under the influence of a tranquilizing drug and that the drug was removed after a one-week period. Do you think he would have become desensitized to many of the threatening or aversive aspects of his daily environment? Would the drug-induced relaxation responses have become conditioned to enough features of his life situation that he would continue to be relatively relaxed without the drug? Why or why not?

Unfortunately, it is difficult to get people to stop taking such drugs long enough to see how well they would be able to cope without them. Perhaps gradual drug withdrawal would facilitate the process. This is often used to reduce the adverse physical effects of withdrawing a person from a hard drug on which he has become physiologically dependent. Can you think of any possible psychological advantages of using gradual withdrawal?

5. Gradual exposure therapy relies primarily upon graded exposure and repetition to bring about an extinction of fear reactions.

Controlled experiments are required to determine whether the special adjunctive use of relaxation responses or feeding responses to directly counteract the anxiety actually enhance the effectiveness of real-life desensitization. If it is not too difficult to incorporate such incompatible responses into the treatment, it might be thought wise to use them anyway. Can you think of any harm which might result from employing such responses in real-life desensitization?

The basic assumption is that these responses and anxiety are mutually incompatible. Suppose that, during Peter's treatment, the rabbit's presence at some point evoked enough anxiety to disturb Peter's eating. Is it possible that the fear responses might thereby become conditioned to the eating situation so that Peter might have anxieties about eating in the same or similar situations in the future?

From the learning theory standpoint, counterposing a threatening stimulus with a neutral one would seem to represent a basic contingency for teaching fear of the neutral stimulus. In view of this, the practitioner should exercise special caution when using a method of real-life desensitization with incompatible responses. How could real-life desensitization with sexual responses have similar adverse side effects?

CHAPTER 8

Social Modeling

Many of our behaviors are partly based on observation and imitation of other people's behavior. New parents are delighted when their child exhibits behaviors which resemble their own—first movements and eventually vocalizations. Perhaps because parents are closely associated with providing most of the infant's comforts, imitating them may develop secondary reinforcing properties for the child even in the parents' absence. The act of imitation, which is a learned behavioral pattern, may then become shaped and refined through selective reinforcement. Thus, the parents' enthusiasm and encouragement when they see the child behaving like them is likely to promote further imitative behavior.

Eventually, many of the behaviors observed and imitated by the child will involve activities which lead directly to positive rewards, for example, turning the radio dial or opening the cookie jar. It is therefore no surprise that the child soon learns that the responses of siblings and adults are a source of information about behaviors which might pay off for him. At the beginning, perhaps the main rewards for imitative behavior are the attention and affection of the person being imitated, but as the child gets older he learns to discriminate and reproduce those functional behaviors which have direct favorable environmental consequences. Observing the behavior of others and its consequences is a much safer and more efficient way of learning about the behavioral contingencies which exist in one's environment than trial and error; this is probably why so much of human behavior originates through social learning processes.

Psychodynamic theorists have noted that an individual often exhibits behaviors similar to those of a significant person in his life. They have formulated such terms as "identification," "introjection," and "incorporation" to conceptualize the underlying processes (see Fenichel, 1945). Miller and Dollard (1941) reported research on several types of imitative learning which were formulated in learning theory terms. Bandura (Bandura and Walters, 1963; Bandura, 1962, 1969, 1971) has further conceptualized the processes of *social modeling,* as he calls it, within a behavioral model. With his associates, Bandura performed numerous experiments to examine the nature of social modeling and its controlling variables, and he has also developed specific methods for use in therapeutic contexts. Bandura's work has had considerable impact on applied behavior modification, and since this is our main interest, we shall proceed with a survey of the formulations and methods based primarily on his writings.

Bandura (1971) identified three basic ways in which observing someone else can influence changes in a person's behavior: teaching new patterns of behavior; eliminating fears and response inhibitions; and facilitating preexisting behavior patterns. These three categories will presently be described and illustrated in their applications to clinical problems.

Observational Learning Effects

Observational learning effects refer to the acquisition of new patterns of behavior resulting from another's demonstration. For example, a woodworking student may learn how to operate an electric jigsaw machine by watching a skilled carpenter. Even though the component hand movements are already in the student's repertoire, their integration into this complex pattern can be greatly facilitated by observing the carpenter. Similarly, a man who has difficulty expressing his romantic desires to a female acquaintance may considerably improve his social exploits by observing demonstrations by his therapist. The appropriate words and emotions are all in the man's repertoire, but the social modeling by the therapist teaches him how to combine them in an appropriate way. When the new behavioral pattern involves some kind of skill, as in the case of the woodworking student or the frustrated suitor, the effectiveness of the performance is likely to improve further with practice or rehearsal.

Bandura (1971) maintains that there are "four interrelated subprocesses that determine whether exposure to the behavior of others will produce new modes of response in observers [p. 657]." These include: (1) attentional processes—the observer must attend to and perceive the behavior of the model and relevant aspects of the stimulus situation; (2) retention processes—the observer must remember and retain the information in imaginal and/or verbal form; (3) motoric reproduction processes—the observer must have within his repertoire the essential component responses and be able to use the symbolic representation of modeled patterns to guide his performance; and (4) reinforcement and motivational processes—the probability of the observer subsequently reproducing the modeled behavior depends upon whether he expects to gain anything by the performance. Bandura (1962) also makes the distinction between the acquisition and the performance of modeled behaviors: a person may acquire specific behavior merely by observing someone else, but he may not perform the behavior himself until the reinforcement contingencies are favorable for him. This suggestion that new response patterns may be learned without actually being performed or rewarded somewhat contrasts to the emphasis placed upon these factors by reinforcement theorists. Of course, the expectation of future utility is likely to guide the individual's attentional processes, so even the acquisition of modeled behavior may not be entirely independent of motivational processes.

An experiment to evaluate the effectiveness of observational learning in increasing social behavior in nursery-school children who

92

tended to withdraw and isolate themselves was performed by O'-Connor (1969) and is adapted here. He referred to his treatment as *symbolic modeling* because the modeled behavior was presented in a film rather than by live demonstration:

> Children in the modeling condition saw a 23-minute sound–color film which portrayed a sequence of 11 scenes in which children interacted in a nursery-school setting. In each episode, a child was shown first observing the interaction of others and then joining in the social activities with favorable results. The other children, for example, would offer him play material, talk to him, smile and generally respond in a positive manner to his advances into the activity. The scenes gradually increased in terms of the vigor of the social activity and the size of the group. The initial scenes involved very calm activities such as sharing a book or toy while two children were seated. In the terminal scenes as many as six children were shown gleefully tossing play equipment around the room. To further accent the modeling cues and the positive consequences associated with the social behavior of the approaching child, a narrative sound track of a woman's voice described the actions of the model and the other children in the ongoing sequence [p. 18].[1]

Six withdrawn children received this symbolic modeling treatment, and their social behavior before and after the treatment was compared to that of seven withdrawn children who observed an unrelated control film on the acrobatic performances of dolphins. The youngsters who had received the symbolic modeling treatment later exhibited a significant increase in their level of social interaction whereas the controls showed no such increase, thus demonstrating the effectiveness of the modeling method.

Lovaas and his coworkers developed a promising methodology for treating autistic or schizophrenic children which incorporates modeling procedures. Autism may be characterized by extreme withdrawal, language deficits, retarded intellectual development, self-destructive behavior, and/or social unresponsiveness. Traditional methods of treatment have proved ineffective in dealing with such disorders, perhaps because those methods rely largely upon

[1]From *Journal of Applied Behavior Analysis,* 1969, **2,** 15–22. Copyright 1969 by the Society for the Experimental Analysis of Behavior, Inc. Used by permission.

verbal interaction and a therapeutic relationship, which cannot be established with these children. Since the development of complex behavior is greatly facilitated through observing such behavior in others, one basic problem with the autistic child is that he does not attend to or imitate other people. The initial task, then, was to develop a method to teach the autistic child to imitate the nonverbal behavior of others and then to use this imitative ability to promote further social and intellectual development in the child.

Lovaas, Freitas, Nelson, and Whalen (1967) described the initial training procedure, which has been adapted here. It was intended to teach the child to imitate a variety of nonverbal tasks or behaviors modeled by an adult:

> The training procedure relied heavily on initial prompting and continuous food reinforcement for correct behavior, and subsequent fading of prompts and shifts to partial reinforcement. Specifically, the adult would engage in a particular behavior, which represents the training or discriminative stimulus. If the child did not exhibit (match) this behavior within five seconds, the adult would prompt the response by doing whatever was necessary and convenient for the child to complete the response. Most often, prompts consisted of physically moving the child through the desired behavior. For example, if the adult demonstrated the placement of a ball in a cup, and the child failed to imitate this, the adult would take the child's hand with the ball and move it towards the cup, and by releasing his grip on the child's hand, cause the ball to fall within the cup. On subsequent trials, the adult would fade the prompt; that is, he would gradually remove his active participation in the child's response. For example, he might gradually lessen his hold on the child's hand, then merely touch the child's hand, then his elbow, then his shoulder, and finally only emit the behavior to be imitated. Reinforcement in the form of small bites of the child's food would be given after correct responses. As training progressed the child's behavior would no longer require prompts but instead would come entirely under the control of the adult's modeling behavior, and the food reinforcement would only be delivered for such unprompted responses [pp. 173–174].[2]

Once the beginnings of imitative behavior have been established, this is used as a base on which to build and expand socially and

[2]Adapted from *Behaviour Research and Therapy,* 1967, **5**, 171–181. Copyright 1967 by Pergamon Press. Used by permission.

intellectually useful behavior. Special emphasis is placed on basic skills such as following rules, personal hygiene, drawing, appropriate sex-role behavior, and nonverbal components of communication such as smiling and head-nodding. The procedure consists of first bringing the new behavior under imitative control and then shifting the control from the adult's modeled behavior to a more appropriate stimulus, such as a verbal command. The same general method is also used for verbal training, first by teaching the child to imitate sounds and words, then to use those words to label corresponding objects and activities, and eventually to develop speech that becomes increasingly more spontaneous and less dependent on external prompting. Lovaas (1969) prepared a film to illustrate the methods he used in teaching language to autistic children; their behavioral changes were often quite dramatic. Although it appears necessary to develop supplementary tactics to promote generalization of the child's newly acquired behaviors to people and situations outside the training setting, Lovaas' approach, with its emphasis upon modeling and reinforcement, has already had considerable impact in the treatment of childhood autism.

Inhibitory and Disinhibitory Effects

Social modeling may be used to strengthen or weaken inhibitions of responses which already exist in a person. By observing the positive or negative consequences of another's behavior in a situation which would be conflictful for the observer, he may become more or less inclined to perform the same behavior himself. For example, a candy machine may pose a frustrating dilemma for a hungry person who has occasionally lost coins in similar machines. Observing the consequences of another person's attempt to operate the machine is likely to influence the first person's decision about risking a try. Similarly, a youngster who is afraid of dogs may observe a playmate approach, pet, and play with a puppy with no bad consequences. This would probably lead to a reduction in the observing youngster's fear, as evidenced in his increased approach to dogs. On the other hand, if the playmate–model had been barked at or bitten by the puppy, the observing youngster would probably have become even more fearful of approaching dogs.

One of the primary therapeutic uses for social modeling is in the elimination of unrealistic fears and the *disinhibition* of associated approach responses. Bandura (1971) reports that, in clinical practice, the most effective strategy for treating phobic fear reactions consists of a program of *participant modeling.* This begins by having a client observe a live model safely interact with the feared objects or situations which are graded in terms of their fear-evoking potential. That is, as in the case of systematic desensitization (see Chapter Five), the feared scenes can be ranked; the model would then perform them beginning with the mildly threatening ones and gradually working up to the more threatening ones. This initial part of the treatment is then followed by a brief program of additional modeling together with guided participation, in which the client is encouraged to perform the same graded activities. In instances where the favorable conditions do not produce the desired behavior, the client may be physically guided in performing the responses, and throughout the process the client's efforts are also socially reinforced with approval and praise. As treatment continues, the amount of demonstration, protection, and guidance may be progressively diminished until the client can encounter the feared situations comfortably and effectively.

Bandura (1971) conceptualized the process of change associated with modeling combined with guided participation as follows:

> Repeated modeling of approach responses, mainly through its informative function, decreases the arousal potential of aversive stimuli below the threshold for activating avoidance responses, thus enabling persons to engage, albeit somewhat anxiously, in approach behavior. Whenever vicarious extinction alone does not restore desired behavior, physical guidance, through its reassuring and protective functions, serves as an additional means of reducing fear arousal and facilitating performance of previously inhibited responses. Direct contact with threats that are no longer objectively justified provides a variety of new experiences which, if favorable, further extinguish residual anxiety and avoidance tendencies. ... After approach behavior toward formerly

avoided objects has been fully restored, the resultant new experiences give rise to substantial reorganization of attitudes [pp. 688–689].[3]

Participant modeling, or *contact desensitization,* as it has also been called (Ritter, 1968), was evaluated in an experiment by Bandura, Blanchard, and Ritter (1969) working with subjects who were afraid of snakes. The following description of the treatment, which combined graduated live modeling with guided participation, was adapted from their report:

After observing intimate snake-interaction behavior repeatedly modeled by the experimenter, subjects were aided through demonstration and joint participation to perform progressively more threatening approach responses toward the king snake. In the initial procedure subjects observed through a one-way mirror the experimenter perform a series of threatening activities with the king snake that provided striking demonstrations that close interaction with the snake does not have harmful consequences. During this period, which lasted approximately 15 minutes, the experimenter held the snake close to his face, allowed it to crawl over his body at will, and let it loose to slither about the room. After returning the snake to its glass cage, the experimenter invited the subject to join him in the room and to be seated in one of four chairs placed at varying distances from the experimenter's chair. The experimenter then removed the snake from the cage and began the treatment with relatively nonthreatening performance tasks and proceeded through increasingly fear-provoking activities. . . .

At each step the experimenter himself exhibited fearless behavior and gradually led subjects into touching, stroking, and then holding the midsection of the snake's body with gloved and then bare hands while the experimenter held the snake securely by the head and tail. Whenever a subject was unable to perform the behavior upon demonstration alone, she was asked to place her hand on the experimenter's and to move her hand down gradually until it touched the snake's body. After subjects no longer felt any apprehension about touching the snake under these secure conditions, anxieties about contact with the snake's head area and entwining tail were extinguished. The experimenter again performed the tasks fearlessly, and then he and the

[3]Adapted from Bandura, A., Psychotherapy based upon modeling principles, from *Handbook of Psychotherapy and Behavior Change: An Empirical Analysis* edited by A. E. Bergin and S. L. Garfield. Copyright © 1971 by John Wiley & Sons, Inc. Reprinted by permission.

subject enacted the responses jointly; as subjects became less fearful the experimenter gradually reduced his participation and control over the snake until eventually subjects were able to hold the snake in their laps without assistance, to let the snake loose in the room and to retrieve it, and to let it crawl freely over their bodies. Progress through the graded approach tasks was paced according to the subjects' apprehensiveness. The threat value of the activities for each subject determined the order in which they were performed. When they reported being able to perform one activity with little or no fear, they were eased into a more difficult interaction. Treatment was terminated when subjects were able to execute all the snake interaction tasks independently [p. 180].[4]

The participant modeling method described above was compared to a symbolic modeling method, in which subjects merely observed a film showing models engaging in progressively more threatening interactions with a snake, and to the imaginal systematic desensitization method which was described in Chapter Five. Subjects who were treated with either of the latter two methods generally showed some improvement, in contrast to control subjects who received no treatment and showed virtually no change. However, the participant modeling treatment proved to be the most effective approach to reducing the snake-phobic behavior, with over 90 percent of the subjects reportedly being cured or very much improved. Participant modeling also proved very efficient in terms of the time required, the average duration of treatment being only two hours and ten minutes distributed over several sessions.

Response Facilitation
Effects

The behaviors of other people often serve as discriminative stimuli in prompting related behaviors in an observer. Here we are referring to response patterns which already exist in the observer's

---

[4]Adapted from Bandura, A., Blanchard, E. B., and Ritter, B., "The relative efficacy of desensitization and modeling approaches for inducing behavioral, affective, and attitudinal changes," *Journal of Personality and Social Psychology,* 1969, **13,** 173–199. Copyright 1969 by the American Psychological Association, and used by permission.

repertoire and are not being inhibited, but which may be prompted by their appropriateness in relation to the behaviors of others in particular situations. For example, when a secretary observes several of her associates get up and start walking toward the refreshment room, this suggests to her that it is coffee-break time and she follows suit. Similarly, a dinner guest observes the other guests placing their napkins on their laps, and this reminds him to do the same. According to Bandura (1971), an individual's responsiveness to modeling influences will depend largely upon three factors. These are, in order of importance, (1) the reinforcement contingencies associated with matching behavior, (2) the personal attributes of the model, and (3) the characteristics of the observer. Thus, if the secretary had not been in the mood for coffee, or if she did not care to spend a few minutes chatting with her associates because there was one in particular she disliked, or if the boss did not appear too pleased about the departure of the other employees, she might have remained at her desk.

Research has suggested that such characteristics as competence, status, and interpersonal warmth increase a person's power to influence the behavior of others through modeling (see Bandura, 1971, pp. 695–696). Furthermore, people who tend to be dependent, lack self-esteem, or feel incompetent are especially likely to pattern their behavior after successful models. Similarity between observer and model in such characteristics as age, sex, race, and socioeconomic status have also been found to promote imitation. Although these factors may be less influential than the reinforcement contingencies in effecting changes in an observer's behavior, they would appear to have some implications for the therapist's behavior in the clinical setting. In particular, since the client is likely to view the therapist as a competent and prestigious person, the client is likely to be particularly vigilant in observing the therapist for clues regarding appropriate behavior. This would suggest that therapists may be able to enhance their effectiveness by modeling response patterns which are directly relevant to the needs of their clients. Such desirable behavior modeled by the therapist, together with the arrangement of favorable consequences contingent upon the client's reproductions, may represent an effective way of promoting improved behavior.

Modeling stimuli can be presented to a person in a variety of ways—live demonstrations, films, verbal instructions, or tape-recordings. J. A. Sherman (1965) used a method of reinforced imitation involving instructions and demonstrations to reinstate verbal behavior in a hospitalized 61-year-old psychotic woman who had not spoken for 33 years. Initial attempts to use shaping and fading techniques to establish some vocal behavior in the woman succeeded only in producing a low rate of emission of very faint sounds, so after 35 such sessions the therapist proceeded as follows (adapted from Sherman, 1965):

The purpose of using an imitative procedure was to attempt to establish a functional class of imitative behavior, such that strengthening imitative nonverbal responses would result in the strengthening of imitative vocal and verbal responses. As a starting point, various nonverbal behaviors of the patient which were under the therapist's verbal control, such as standing up, sitting down, and picking up a spoon, were used. If the subject performed the requested response she was reinforced with a bite of food and "Good" from the therapist. Gradually, two aspects of the procedure were changed: first, the verbal description of the action was dropped until the therapist merely said "Do this" and demonstrated the response to be imitated; second, the responses exhibited by the therapist were gradually changed until they became more and more similar to vocal behavior. By session 45 (the tenth session of reinforced imitation) the patient was reliably imitating several sounds vocalized by the therapist, and by session 57 she was consistently imitating a variety of simple words said by the therapist. A fading procedure was then employed to teach her to use the words to label the corresponding objects, and gradually she learned to respond with appropriate words to name specific foods. In fact, some of the words which appeared in her repertoire had never been directly shaped by the therapist. By the end of session 99 the patient was consistently naming scores of objects. She also was responding regularly with appropriate replies to simple questions and statements made by the therapist, although her replies generally consisted only of one or two words [pp. 160–162].[5]

[5]Adapted from Sherman, J. A., "Use of reinforcement and imitation to reinstate verbal behavior in mute psychotics," *Journal of Abnormal Psychology,* 1965, **70,** 155–164. Copyright 1965 by the American Psychological Association, and used by permission.

100

WEST HILLS COLLEGE LIBRARY
COALINGA, CALIFORNIA

Although the woman did not become a fluent conversationalist, the reinstatement of speech brought about by reinforced imitation still represented a tremendous improvement after 33 years of virtual silence.

Issues to Consider

1. The participant modeling method for treating phobic reactions consists of several component procedures, each of which may be of some benefit. For example, the method furnishes the client with information about the feared objects or situations, it shows him a model interacting with the feared situations in a graded series without any bad consequences, and it provides actual contact with the series of feared situations including practice in performing the appropriate responses. How would you go about designing an experiment to determine the relevance of these factors? Which of the factors do you think would be found most important, or do you think they are inseparably dependent upon one another?

2. In Bandura's conceptualization of the process of change associated with modeling, he stated (see p. 96) that "After approach behavior toward formerly avoided objects has been fully restored, the resultant new experiences give rise to substantial reorganization of attitudes." In other words, he is suggesting that an individual's attitudes toward feared objects or situations can be changed by first changing his behavior toward those situations through modeling. Traditionally-oriented clinicians generally attempt to treat people with phobic reactions by helping them gain insight into the irrational reasons for their fears, assuming that this new understanding will change their attitudes, which will then change their behavior. Do you think that a change in behavior can lead to a change in attitudes, that a change in attitudes can lead to a change in behavior, or that both can occur?

If you think it would depend upon the problem, which approach would you recommend in working with a client who is afraid of insects?

Which approach would you recommend in working with a client who is afraid of failure or being rejected?

If you recommended a modeling approach for the person who is afraid of failure, how would you do it?

3. Because of his perceived competence and status, the therapist might exert strong modeling influences over his clients' behavior. Traditionally-oriented clinicians often tend to assume a somewhat distant posture in which they focus upon interpreting the client's verbal productions and attempt to conceal their own feelings and reactions. What effect do you think such a posture will have in terms of its modeling influences upon the client?

Would there be any favorable consequences for the client in dealing with present and future behavioral difficulties?

Since such a modeling influence would appear to emphasize thought rather than action, do you think its value would depend upon the nature of the problem being confronted?

4. The behavior therapist may model specific behavior patterns to teach the client how to deal with specific problem situations, but he may also intentionally use his influential position to model a general approach for identifying and coping with behavioral problems (see Ullmann, 1969). If the client can learn such a general strategy for confronting problems, perhaps he may be able to function as his own therapist when he encounters new problems. What do you think of this possibility?

Ullmann (1969) also emphasizes that the therapist should not begin by modeling the optimal target performance; instead, he should shape toward the goal and gradually fade his prompts. Why do you think this might be important?

5. All therapists tend to reveal some of their personal views and values to their clients, either intentionally or unintentionally. Assuming that these exert some modeling influence over the clients, do you think it is a desirable phenomenon?

If some of the therapist's values conflict with those of the client in areas unrelated to the focus of the treatment, do you think that this might create additional problems for the client?

102

Are there ways the modeling influence of the therapist's personal views might be reduced or avoided?

6. Token economy systems (see p. 42) have promoted dramatic changes in the daily behaviors of large groups of patients. However, Bandura (1971) appropriately points out that variations in social behavior in such situations may not be entirely due to the direct effects of the programmed reward contingencies. Instead, the changed behavior in some of the patients may be partially a consequence of modeling influences emanating from the behavior of other patients (who may be responding to the newly programmed reinforcement contingencies). From the practical therapeutic standpoint, the administrators may not be particularly concerned whether the improvements result directly from the reinforcement conditions or from modeling influences. Can you think of any reason why they should care about this, or does the issue appear to be of merely theoretical interest?

Suppose a token economy system were well-designed, but a few influential patients repeatedly diverted the attention of other patients by continuing to model undesirable behavior. Administrators who were not aware of the relevance of modeling influences might inappropriately attribute the failure to presumed inadequacies in the token economy itself, which might lead them to introduce changes in that with no greater promise of success. Since you know some of the theory and understand the possibilities, what would you recommend to the administrators?

CHAPTER 9

Expressive Training

Western society emphasizes and provides for the training of behaviors associated with intellectual and physical mastery of the environment, but it makes little systematic attempt to train youngsters in basic social or expressive skills. In fact, the available models —such as parents, siblings, teachers, and friends—often exhibit inconsistent or inappropriate characteristics and standards of social behavior, and the environmental consequences of interpersonal behaviors are also often difficult to ascertain. It is therefore no surprise that social inhibitions and ineffectuality are among the most common sources of psychological distress in the adult. Many individuals have difficulty expressing their thoughts and feelings in interpersonal situations requiring expression of friendliness or affection, verbalization of requests or refusal of unreasonable requests, admission of error or fault, assertion of displeasure or anger, and so on. Consequently, such people often fail to achieve basic social goals and experience anxiety and low self-esteem. *Expressive training* refers to several related methods designed to help a person become more socially at ease and develop effective interpersonal skills for behaving spontaneously and appropriately in social contexts.

Many behavioral problems require such treatment. A successful businessman is quite adept socially, but becomes completely overwhelmed with anxiety when he must deliver a speech to a large group of his colleagues. A college sophomore has always been timid and shy, with no dates in high school; he is still unable to ask a girl for a date, nor would he know what to do if his invitation were accepted. An attractive and competent girl in her early twenties has been depicted by her friends as cold and aloof; she finds it difficult to express affectionate feelings toward people, and her boyfriend complains that she holds back her thoughts and emotions from him. A young salesman frequently feels picked on by the store manager who appears to embarrass him intentionally in front of other employees and customers; the young man gets very nervous whenever the manager is around and does not know how to handle the situation. A freshman is living in a dormitory, and an older student frequently barges into her room and starts relating her problems; the freshman is annoyed by this distraction, and it often interferes with her work, but she does not know how to end these unwanted and unpleasant visits. An executive secretary runs an efficient office, vigilantly watching over her staff and keeping them busy; yet, she cannot understand why these people, whom she regards as her friends, do not wait for her to join them for lunch and do not invite her to their parties. A man in his thirties has always had difficulty asserting himself when he is slighted; for example, when someone steps in front of him in a line, when the food he is served in a restaurant is not what he ordered, or when he purchases an item which is later found to be defective, he experiences a great deal of anger and resentment but is unable to stand up for his rights.

Most people have had similar experiences; individuals vary in the ease and effectiveness with which they handle them. Usually, as we get older, we become more socially comfortable and interpersonally effective. However, perhaps because of adverse environmental circumstances, some people continue to experience unrealistic social anxieties or inhibitions or to exhibit maladaptive ways of behaving in various social contexts, while others who generally appear to be socially at ease and proficient encounter new situations in which they find themselves interpersonally ineffectual.

Lack of interpersonal skills often accompanies the presence of social anxieties or inhibitions; they influence each other. The anxiety evoked in interpersonal contexts is likely to interfere with the expression of appropriate feelings and adaptive performance, thus restricting the behavioral repertoire of the individual and minimizing his impact on others and on his environment. Likewise, unsatisfactory or embarrassing social experiences may leave the individual emotionally distressed by his unexpressed feelings and anxious about his personal ineffectuality. Here we are concerned not only with the individual who has difficulty expressing displeasure or anger but also with the individual who has difficulty expressing friendly and affectionate feelings. Therefore, the generic term "expressive training" is used in preference to "assertive training," which seems more circumscribed.

The therapist's expressive training interventions are generally designed to encourage every impulse in the client toward expressing the inhibited responses (see Salter, 1949) and to teach him the appropriate responses if they are not already in his behavioral repertoire. Each performance of expressive responses is assumed to lead to a weakening of the inhibiting anxiety, provided there are no adverse consequences. In fact, if the newly expressed responses are appropriate to the circumstances, positive instrumental consequences related to adequacy and control in social situations are likely to reinforce the adaptive responses. The extinction of anxiety and the concomitant reinforcement of the instrumental expressive responses thus complement and facilitate each other.

In some cases the inhibiting anxiety may be so great that no amount of prompting can get the person actually to try out mild versions of self-expression in real social contexts. In such instances the therapist may initially focus directly on the anxiety and use an imaginal desensitization method to reduce the inhibiting social anxieties to the point where beginning efforts at self-expression become possible. In other cases, the problem may represent a lack of social skills rather than inhibiting anxieties. In these instances the therapist would attempt to teach the client the appropriate things to say and do in the various social contexts that prove difficult for him.

The nature of the client's interpersonal anxieties and inadequacies are often revealed in initial interviews. As the client relates his problems to the therapist he may mention experiences in which he was dominated or exploited by relatives, friends, employers, salesmen, or strangers, but took no appropriate counteraction. Likewise, he may describe situations in which he felt friendly toward another person, but was too timid to express his affectionate feelings. Additional inhibitions or deficiencies in social skill may be revealed in the client's responses on personality questionnaires. Information gathered from all of these sources and from the client's actual behavior during initial interviews should enable the therapist to decide whether expressive training is needed and, if so, in what contexts.

Having decided to use expressive training procedures, the therapist proceeds to explore with the client the general nature and undesirable effects of inhibitions of self-expression in social situations. The therapist may provide examples that show the inappropriateness and irrationality of excessive interpersonal inhibitions. Such examples may also illustrate the desirable consequences of appropriate social expressiveness, both immediate (interpersonal effectiveness, achievement of objectives, respect of others) and long-term (emotional well-being, self-confidence, self-respect).

The therapist will then shift the focus to the client's own problems of interpersonal ineffectuality, attempting to help the client recognize the nature of his difficulties and the appropriateness and desirability of his becoming more expressive in specific social situations and relationships. Such discussions generally arouse enough personal dissatisfaction and motivation for change in the client that he can partially overcome the restraints of his social anxieties and begin to try out appropriate expressive responses. In working with an individual whose interpersonal inertia is partially related to strong moralistic training, the therapist may attempt logical arguments to convince him of the appropriateness of standing up for his rights even when it may involve hurting the feelings of the people who are taking advantage of him.

Ordinarily, the therapist will briefly explain the theoretical rationale underlying the expressive training procedures in terms the client can understand. In essence, the client may be told that the outward expression of his feelings will tend to counteract the anxiety he feels. Then, with repeated occasions of social assertiveness accompanied by instruction, the anxiety responses will progressively decrease in strength while the interpersonally expressive responses will increase in strength because of their favorable consequences. To some extent, it is a matter of learning by doing, for "nothing succeeds like success."

The client must be taught to distinguish appropriate expressive responses from the undesirable extremes of excessively inhibited reactions on the one hand and overly aggressive responses on the other. This may be done by discussing the client's own past experiences, by case illustrations, or by examples from the therapist's experience. To initiate the actual treatment, the client is asked to describe several mildly threatening interpersonal situations from his own experience, the appropriate expressive responses are identified, and the client is encouraged to try out mild attempts at such self-assertion in these situations as he encounters them in the future. In the early stages of training the goal is to achieve the expression, albeit somewhat clumsy, of the previously inhibited feelings. The client should gradually gain a sense of control and adequacy in several mild situations; this will extend into more and more challenging situations, and his social competence and self-confidence will increase accordingly. Eventually, he will become able to size up a social situation accurately and express himself appropriately.

Clients undergoing expressive training are often asked to keep accurate notes of all significant interpersonal experiences during the course of treatment. These notes would include the circumstances surrounding each experience, the client's feelings at the time, how he reacted, the effects of his response, his feelings right after the experience, and his retrospective appraisal of the event. In addition to compelling the client to pay careful attention to his interpersonal encounters and his reactions, the notes assist the therapist in identifying specific difficulties.

When the client's repertoire of interpersonal responses is found to be deficient or inappropriate, that is, when he does not appear to have the requisite social skills for behaving appropriately, play-acting of appropriate responses is often found helpful. This procedure, known as *behavior rehearsal,* has much in common with such methods as psychodrama (Moreno, 1946, 1969), role-playing (Kelly, 1955), and social modeling (Bandura, 1971; see also Chapter 8 of this book). The client is instructed to reenact past experiences, or act out anticipated future experiences, while the therapist plays the role of the other person. The therapist may then switch roles and act the part of the client. Initially, he will show the client how the client appears when he behaves ineffectively, and then he will demonstrate appropriate expressive behavior which functions as a model for the client in learning the adaptive responses by imitation.

Lazarus (Wolpe and Lazarus, 1966) reports that:

> Most assertive trainees seem to follow a similar pattern of evolution. First, there is an increased awareness of their non-assertiveness and its negative repercussions. This is followed by an intellectual appreciation of assertive behavior and its positive effects. Increasing distaste for their own ineffectuality and resentment towards the forces which seem to be maintaining or reinforcing the non-assertiveness soon lead to tentative, usually clumsy attempts at self-assertive responses. If positive effects ensue, the probability of engaging in more assertive behavior increases. Occasionally, as emotional satisfactions intensify and spread, previously timid and dominated individuals tend to overassert themselves. Negative environmental feedback combined with the monitoring of the therapist results in the necessary toning down of these responses. The patient learns to be dominant without being dominating. Assertion for the sake of assertion—a useful drill at an early stage—gives way to discriminative, adjustive responses. Finally, as the patient becomes aware of his growing mastery of interpersonal situations, there develops a genuine and fitting indifference to minor slights, petty machinations, small irrationalities and other insignificant "pin-pricks" of daily interaction [p. 47].

The following case treated by Lazarus (Wolpe and Lazarus, 1966) illustrates several of the procedures used in expressive training:

> Mr. P. R., aged 38 years, complained of depression and described himself as an "occupational misfit." Although highly qualified in accountancy and economics, he held only junior positions in his work. He stated that he felt frustrated and demoralized. At the time that he sought behavior therapy, he had received promotion to the position of Assistant Chief Ledger Clerk in a large organization. This slight elevation in status, utterly absurd for a man with his excellent qualifications, tended to reactivate his personal misgivings about his station in life, and led him to treatment "as a last resort."

During the initial interview it became clear that Mr. P. R. was grossly deficient in assertive behavior. The therapist lent him a copy of Salter's (1949) "Conditioned Reflex Therapy" and advised him to prepare a critique of selected chapters for his next session, a week later. The patient returned for his second session having carried out his initial assignment and stated that he felt hopeless about his future. "That chapter on inhibition made me feel that Salter had made a special study of me before writing it. . . . I don't see how it is possible for a leopard to change its spots." The therapist provided a good deal of encouragement and reassurance but cautioned Mr. P. R. to make haste slowly. At the next session, the patient stated that promotion at work was a *sine qua non* for the acquisition of assertive habits. "I feel that until I am properly fixed up at work we will both be wasting our time." The therapist stressed that Mr. P. R.'s lack of assertiveness was responsible for his occupational failures, and that vocational advancement would have to follow rather than precede increased assertiveness. It was clear, however, that Mr. P. R. would use the work situation as the sole criterion for gauging his general improvement. A careful analysis showed that opportunities for advancement in his firm were extremely limited. It was obvious that Mr. P. R. would have to go elsewhere to achieve the desired elevation in occupational status, but he rationalized that he would feel less secure in an unfamiliar work milieu. Further enquiries revealed that Mr. P. R. abhorred the idea of being interviewed by prospective employers. This area was then made the focus of attention for assertive training by means of behavior rehearsal.

Mr. P. R. was told to pretend that the therapist was a prominent business executive who had advertised for an experienced accountant to take charge of one of his companies. Mr. P. R. had applied for the position and had been asked to present himself for an interview. The therapist instructed Mr. P. R. to leave the consulting room, to knock on the door and to enter when invited to do so.

At the therapist's deliberately resonant "come in!" Mr. P. R. opened the door of the consulting room and hesitantly approached the desk. The therapist interrupted the role-playing procedure to mirror the patient's timid posture, shuffling gait, downcast eyes and overall tension. Mr. P. R. was required to sit at the desk and to play the role of the prominent business executive while the therapist re-enacted Mr. P. R.'s entry into the room. The patient was asked to criticize the therapist's performance. The therapist then modeled the entry of an "assertive individual," asking the patient to note the impact of variations in posture and gait and the all-important absence or presence of eye-contact.

The "correct" entry was rehearsed several times until Mr. P. R.'s approach to the prominent-executive-behind-the-desk was completely

110

devoid of any overt signs of timidity or anxiety. He was then taught to deal with a variety of entries—being met at the door; the employer who makes himself incommunicado while studying important-looking documents; and the overeffusive one who self-consciously tries to place him at ease.

Next, the content of the interview was scrutinized. Mr. P. R.'s replies to questions concerning his background, qualifications and experience were tape-recorded. Mr. P. R. was instructed to place himself in the position of the prospective employer and asked to decide whether or not he would employ the applicant on the basis of his recorded interview. It was clear from the recording that the elimination of Mr. P. R.'s hesitant gait and posture had not generalized to his faltering speech. Above all, it was noted that Mr. P. R. tended to undersell himself. Instead of stressing his excellent qualifications he mumbled rather incoherent and unimpressive generalities about his background and training. The therapist demonstrated more efficient verbal responses which the patient was required to imitate. In this manner, Mr. P. R. was able to rehearse adequate replies to specific questions and to prepare an impressive-sounding discourse for use in unstructured interviews.

The above-mentioned procedures were employed during five therapeutic sessions held at weekly intervals. Mr. P. R. cancelled his sixth appointment and did not communicate for approximately two months. He then made another appointment. On entering the consulting room, he said, "You are looking at the Chief Accountant of . . ." (a very large industrial organization). He then described how he had replied to the advertisement, been exposed to three separate interviews ("You would have been proud of your handiwork. . . . I handled them with such aplomb!") and how he was finally offered the post at an even higher salary than advertised.

Mr. P. R. proclaimed himself "cured." Although the therapist felt that many remaining facets of Mr. P. R.'s interpersonal dealings warranted additional assertive training, he did not discourage him from terminating therapy (on the understanding that he was free to resume should he ever deem it necessary).

Five years later Mr. P. R. telephoned the therapist to report that he had become principal economic advisor to an important mining concern [pp. 48–50].

Lazarus (1966) regards behavior rehearsal as "a specific procedure which aims to replace deficient or inadequate social or interpersonal responses by efficient and effective behavior patterns. The patient achieves this by practicing the desired forms of behavior under the direction and supervision of the therapist [p. 209]" using role-playing and role-reversal techniques. In a clinical context, Lazarus attempted to evaluate the efficacy of this method and compare it with two other commonly used techniques in the treatment of specific interpersonal problems.

Patients who had received no previous treatment and who brought specific social and/or interpersonal difficulties to the attention of the therapist, regardless of their overall problems and primary reasons for seeking therapy, were treated for these specific problems by one of the three procedures. Patients were arbitrarily assigned to treatment by either reflection–interpretation, direct advice, or behavior rehearsal; the experiment ended when 25 patients had been treated by each of the three procedures. When patients presented more than one specific problem area, the most pressing difficulty was selected for initial treatment. A maximum of four 30-minute sessions was devoted to each treated problem; if there was no evidence of change or learning within the one month, the treatment was regarded as having failed. The criterion of change or learning was the presence of objective evidence that the patient was behaving adaptively in the area which had previously constituted a problem.

Whereas 92 percent of the 25 patients treated by behavior rehearsal were found to show evidence of positive learning, only 32 percent of those treated by reflection–interpretation and 44 percent of those treated by direct advice showed such improvement. Twenty-seven of the 31 patients not benefiting from the latter two procedures were then treated by means of behavior rehearsal, and 22 (81 percent) of these subsequently showed improvement. Although there were experimental limitations related to the fact that all three therapeutic procedures were administered by the experimenter, the finding that behavior rehearsal promoted improvement in more than 90 percent of the patients is impressive.

Clinical methods for expressive training such as the behavior rehearsal studied above tend to incorporate various combinations of procedural components, which include such factors as:

1. *Reducing Anxiety.* It may be necessary to reduce or counteract social anxieties which inhibit the client's expression of his thoughts and feelings. For example, the therapist could use a method of imaginal desensitization or arouse strong assertive feelings

through appeals to the client's personal right to be more self-expressive.

2. *Discrimination Training.* A socially naive or inexperienced person may require training in how to make finer discriminations in sizing up social situations. For example, the therapist might discuss and analyze the subtleties of situations of increasing complexity which the client has encountered or expects to encounter.

3. *Information.* In order to teach the client what constitutes adaptive social behavior, the therapist may present information concerning alternative behavior patterns which would be appropriate in particular social situations and label their important features to make them more salient. For example, the therapist may demonstrate or model effective ways to handle increasingly challenging situations and discuss and pay special attention to such response dimensions as verbal content, affective tone, and facial expression.

4. *Rehearsal.* The development of basic social skills and spontaneity in their performance may be facilitated if the client rehearses appropriate response patterns in the nonthreatening environment of the treatment setting. For example, he could role-play responses to representative situations which are graded in the degree to which they require increasing social proficiency.

5. *Feedback.* Rehearsing adaptive response patterns may lead to increasingly proficient behavior if the client receives feedback on the adequacy of each rehearsed performance. For example, he might watch a video tape-recording of his behavior, while the therapist comments on the strong and weak points of the performance along important response dimensions.

6. *Performance.* Since the ultimate objective of any treatment program is to bring about real-life improvement, it may be appropriate to encourage the client to perform the new expressive responses in real situations outside the treatment setting. For example, the client might attempt a graded sequence of realistic interpersonal encounters during his daily activities; the therapist would

instruct him to size up each situation and behave in an appropriately spontaneous and expressive manner.

The complexity of interpersonal or expressive behavior patterns is demonstrated in the variety of factors involved. For example, knowledge of the content and manner of expression of a response pattern may be basic to its mastery, rehearsal and feedback may play important parts in refining it, and favorable environmental contingencies may determine its probability of future occurrence in real situations. The various interpersonal problems and deficiencies presented by different clients may require emphasis upon different treatment procedures. Despite the clinical importance of interpersonal ineffectuality and the desirability of refining and integrating the components in a program of expressive training which will be optimally effective for each individual client, few systematic attempts have been made to assess experimentally the procedural components.

McFall and Marston (1970) developed a laboratory analog of behavior rehearsal which used tape-recordings of challenging social situations. The participants, nonassertive college students, were given individual practice in responding assertively to these situations. Following each rehearsal response, some students received feedback by listening to a recording of their response; other students spent an equivalent amount of time thinking about their response. Then each student evaluated his response according to a prepared outline of performance criteria. The behavior rehearsal treatment, in which students worked alone for four sessions, emphasized rehearsal and self-evaluation, with or without recorded feedback, to improve assertive behavior.

Behavior rehearsal was then compared to a no-treatment control group and to a four-session placebo therapy control group in which a therapist discussed each student's nonassertive behavior with him and encouraged him to behave more assertively. Students who had received behavior rehearsal showed more improvement on behavioral ratings, self-reports of anxiety, and pulse rate than did students in the combined control groups. There was also a nonsignificant indication that the favorable effects of behavior rehearsal may be augmented by providing recorded feedback. Overall, the results suggest that a semiautomated procedure involving the rehearsal and self-evaluation of assertive responses may be helpful in improving assertive performance.

Other research studies have suggested the value of expressive training approaches which include self-reinforcement while confronting a hierarchy of real-life situations (Rehm and Marston, 1968), live modeling plus directed role-playing (Friedman, 1971), and a combination of covert response rehearsal, symbolic verbal modeling, and therapist coaching (McFall and Lillesand, 1971). Additional research is needed to develop further and refine expressive training methods which can be employed educationally with young people to teach basic interpersonal skills before any difficulties are encountered (Sherman, 1971), and therapeutically with adults already experiencing problems associated with interpersonal ineffectuality.

Issues to Consider

1. "Expressive training" here refers to several related procedures designed to help a person become more interpersonally comfortable and skillful. These procedures emphasize such factors as reducing anxiety, discrimination training, presenting information, conducting rehearsal, providing feedback, and encouraging real-life performance. How would you design a research program to determine which combinations of factors are required for promoting the various behaviors which constitute interpersonal expressiveness?

As you may have discovered, one of the difficulties in formulating such research is to specify the behavioral objectives adequately and select measures to assess them. For any specific situation, a variety of expressive response patterns may be equally appropriate and effective. Such variables as the age, sex, social class, and basic personality characteristics might determine which ways are most natural and appropriate for a given person. How would you handle this issue of individual differences in specifying and measuring behavioral objectives in your research program?

Since the ultimate goal of treatment is real-life improvement, how would you assess the effectiveness of expressive behaviors in real social situations?

What do you think would be the main findings of your research program?

2. Unlike some other behavior modification methods, the theoretical foundations of expressive training are often difficult to conceptualize in terms of basic learning principles because of the complexity of the component procedures. For example, an effective expressive response involves several parallel response dimensions including verbal content, affective tone, and facial expression; teaching verbal content (by modeling and rehearsal) involves mechanisms of cognitive information processing and verbal learning which are not yet entirely understood. Can you think of any other aspects of expressive training which would be difficult to formulate theoretically?

The relationship between theory and practice is a two-way street, for often the consequences of a therapeutic intervention provide information which improves our theoretical understanding. Do you recall any examples of this in our consideration of other methods of behavior modification?

3. The term "interpersonal effectiveness" includes a person's ability to size up a social situation accurately, the appropriateness of his feelings, and his skills and effectiveness in expressing them and relating to other people. The newborn infant seems to have none of these behaviors in his repertoire, but in the course of his childhood and adolescence, he gradually learns the behavior patterns which make him a social being. What do you think are the main factors which contribute to social learning?

Perhaps if you think back to your own childhood, you may discover additional clues concerning the factors responsible for social development. Many people can remember trying to imitate the behaviors of children they admired, and some may even recall younger children who tried to imitate them. Observing other people interact and then imitating them is probably one important way in which the child acquires interpersonal skills (see Chapter 8, "Social Modeling"). Do you think there may also be some biological predisposition built in to the human species which makes man a social animal?

How would you investigate such a possibility?

116

4. If children do learn many social behaviors through imitation or modeling, it is easy to understand how interpersonal difficulties can develop. Some children may not be exposed to effective social models who exhibit an array of interpersonal skills, and others may be exposed to models who exhibit maladaptive social behavior—for example, people who are overly aggressive or hostile, excessively passive, or who cannot express love and affection. The child's social environment, particularly his family and friends, would seem to be a very important influence on the development of his attitudes toward people and his ways of relating to them. Western society generally assumes responsibility for the academic education of its children, rather than leaving it entirely in the hands of the family and friends. Do you think we should also try to promote development of social skills in our children by creating large-scale training programs for that purpose?

If so, do you think such programs should be required of all children, for example, by incorporating them into the existing public school systems, or should they be available through private schools in which interested parents could enroll their children for specialized courses? Why?

5. The complexity of the expressive training procedures and the therapist's requisite skills would appear to set serious manpower limits on making such treatment available to those who might benefit from it. At present, few people can pursue individual expressive training because there is a limited number of qualified practitioners. One possibility might be to increase manpower by teaching socially skilled nonprofessionals how to administer expressive training procedures under the supervision of a professional clinician. Another possibility might be to use sound recordings, video tapes, and films to provide standardized social models of effective interpersonal behavior as demonstrations to clients and to provide feedback concerning their own behavior. Since there are often several appropriate and equally effective ways of handling a given social situation, such recorded demonstrations could provide a few of the alternatives. Because of the widespread prevalence of social anxieties and deficiencies in interpersonal skills, the development of such treatment innovations would seem very desirable—as would the reduction in

117

clients' cost that would result from automated methods and para-professional staffing. Can you think of any other ways in which the procedures and their administration might be changed and improved to increase the availability and effectiveness of expressive training?

·

CHAPTER 10

Aversion Therapy

Aversion therapy refers to behavioral methods which emphasize using aversive events or noxious stimulation to treat maladaptive behavior. Aversive contingencies play a prominent role in shaping and controlling much of our behavior; for example, we learn not to walk in traffic, not to eat dirt, and not to tell people exactly what we think of them because of their dangerous or unpleasant consequences. Likewise, we test the water before entering the shower to avoid getting burned or chilled; we tell an acquaintance that we have another commitment rather than that we don't want to see him; we drive within the speed limit (or we watch for highway patrolmen) to avoid getting a traffic ticket; we contrive or exaggerate an explanation for turning in an overdue report to avoid criticism for our lateness. In fact, even when we appear to perform certain behaviors to achieve specific positive rewards, we may actually do them partly to avoid the aversive consequences of not doing them. For example, we work not only to earn money but also to avoid the helpless situation of being without money; likewise, we study not only to gain knowledge but also to avoid the consequences of getting poor grades. In addition to playing an important part in controlling man's behavior in the natural environment, aversive factors can be systematically manipulated to modify maladaptive behavior within the context of a treatment setting.

Although aversive contingencies can control behavior in many ways, they are used in therapy in two primary ways. One form of aversion therapy, which involves *punishment,* is designed to suppress undesirable instrumental behavior by introducing aversive consequences whenever the behavior occurs. For example, if a child continues to ride his new tricycle over the flowers after being told not to, his mother may attempt to stop this by spanking him, by taking his tricycle away for awhile, or by sending him to his room. The other major form of aversion therapy, which involves *classical aversive conditioning,* is designed to make a pleasurable (but undesirable) stimulus object less attractive by pairing it with a noxious stimulus. For example, a person with chronic bronchitis may be administered an electric shock each time he inhales a cigarette in order to make smoking less attractive to him. The processes involved in these two therapeutic uses of aversive contingencies have considerable overlap, although they differ in whether they emphasize associating aversive events with responses or with stimulus objects. The approaches will now be considered in more detail.

Punishment

As indicated above, one form of aversion therapy focuses upon the suppression of undesired instrumental responses through punishment. This consists essentially of introducing some aversive event immediately after the occurrence of the undesired behavior until the individual learns to avoid the aversive consequence by not performing the behavior. Only the undesired response is followed by aversive consequences, so the undesired response's probability of emission is likely to decrease while other responses become more probable. Assuming that some of these responses are appropriate to the situation, they will then continue to be performed because of their adaptive reinforcing consequences. In fact, the long-term success of such a treatment program depends largely on the existence of contingencies which positively reinforce adaptive responses as preferred alternatives to the undesired response which is suppressed.

For example, a child in a nursery school may spend much of his time throwing blocks and other objects around the play area and against the wall and the furnishings. Besides being destructive and dangerous, this behavior is undesirable because it means the child spends little time acquiring new skills through constructive play activities with other children. Although the staff might try to extinguish the behavior by ignoring it, the social reinforcement provided by the attention of the other children might still be sufficient to maintain it. Also, if the child begins to try harder to get the attention of the staff by throwing blocks at the other children, the staff will have to intervene, thereby reinforcing the worst versions of the behavior they are trying to extinguish. In such a situation, it might be more effective to introduce some strong aversive consequence whenever the child throws something in order to bring about a rapid suppression of the undesirable behavior. Provided that the negative effects outweigh the positive effects of this behavior, the child will stop throwing things and will begin to engage in other activities. Some of these new behaviors, such as coloring or playing games, would have adaptive and rewarding consequences, including praise from the staff, which would help establish them as preferred alternatives to throwing things and further increase their probability of emission in the future.

Three basic punishment methods can provide aversive consequences when an undesired response occurs. One method is to administer a noxious stimulus directly; this we shall call *noxious punishment* to distinguish it from the other methods. For example, a painful spanking when the child threw something would constitute a noxious punishment. A second method is to remove a positive reinforcement; this is called *response cost*. For example, taking away the child's favorite toy truck or telling him he could not go out to the playground later would constitute a response cost. The third method is calmly to remove the subject from all sources of reinforcement by placing him in an isolated setting for awhile; this is called *time-out*. For example, placing the child alone for several minutes in an empty

121

room which provided no opportunities for play or attention would constitute a time-out. The nature of the situation, prior experiences with a particular subject, and personal preferences of the treatment administrator would probably determine which procedure would be used.

The following case, adapted from a report by Tate and Baroff (1966), illustrates the use of response cost and then noxious punishment to control a child's self-injurious behavior:

> Sam was an institutionalized nine-year-old psychotic boy who was partially blind. For about five years he had been performing self-injurious behavior which included banging his head against walls and other hard objects, punching his face and head with his fists, and hitting his shoulder with his chin. The head-banging posed a serious threat to completely blinding him. Periodic observations of Sam revealed that he was emitting an average of about two self-injurious responses per minute.
>
> Sam appeared to enjoy physical contact with people and did not like being left alone. This was made the basis for the first attempt at controlling his self-injurious behavior. Treatment sessions consisted of 20-minute walks around the grounds with Sam walking between two experimenters, holding onto a hand of each one. Whenever Sam hit himself, the experimenters pulled their hands away so that he had no physical contact with them, and discontinued any talking. After three seconds, they allowed Sam to grasp their hands again, and the walk resumed. In contrast to control days when the experimenters merely ignored Sam's self-injurious behaviors during their walks, there was a dramatic reduction in the frequency of such behaviors on the experimental days when hand contact was withdrawn. It was also noted that, in contrast to the control days, on experimental days Sam appeared to attend more to environmental stimuli, did not cry, and often smiled.
>
> According to the experimenters, "Although the self-injurious behavior could be reduced by response-contingent withdrawal of physical contact, it was decided that the risk of destroying the right retina by further head-banging was great enough to preclude the long-term use of this method [p. 284]." They then proceeded to use a stock prod to deliver painful electric shocks of brief duration to Sam's lower right leg when he exhibited self-injurious responses in his room. At the same time, noninjurious behaviors were praised. During the first 90-minute period in which shocks were immediately administered contingent on self-injurious responses only five such responses were emitted. During subsequent days the rate of self-injurious responses continued to decline, he did not have to be restrained as much in bed, and there were

122

also favorable side effects: increased spontaneity in play activities and improved eating. At the time of the report, which was 167 days after shock punishment was introduced, the authors indicated that Sam had not been observed to exhibit a self-injurious response for the preceding 20 days [pp. 281–285].[1]

Although it may sometimes be appropriate to use punishment procedures to suppress undesirable behavior, occasional problems should be kept in mind. First of all, unless alternative responses have more favorable consequences within the situation, the undesired responses are likely to remain suppressed only when the person who administered the punishment is around. For example, if a mother punishes her little boy for taking a toy from his sister, this may not reduce the chances of him taking her toys when his mother is not around. The use of punishment also provides a model for the subject in demonstrating the effective use of force to control another's behavior. Thus, in the above example, the boy may then use force to impose his will on other, smaller children. Another undesirable side effect of the use of punishment is that it may make the subject see the punisher in a negative light. For example, if the mother often punishes to control her children's behavior, they are likely to learn to fear her and view her as a potentially threatening person. Nevertheless, sometimes, as in Sam's case, punishment procedures are required, and awareness of possible problems should enable the therapist to minimize adverse side effects.

Classical Aversive Conditioning

The other form of aversion therapy emphasizes the use of noxious stimulation to promote an actual aversion to the objects associated with certain maladaptive behaviors. The target behaviors in classical aversive conditioning are frequently of the chronic bad habit variety which, despite immediate pleasurable effects, are undesirable because of their long-term harmful effects. Excessive smok-

[1]Adapted from *Behaviour Research and Therapy,* 1966, **4,** 281–287. Copyright 1966 by Pergamon Press. Used by permission.

ing, alcohol drinking, or eating would constitute such maladaptive habits. Since most of these responses are initially reinforcing (at least prior to the sore throat, hangover, or guilt feelings), therapy uses classical conditioning to create an actual aversion to the stimulus objects or situations by pairing them with noxious stimuli such as emetic (nausea-inducing) drugs or electric shock. Then, if the individual becomes inclined to perform the maladaptive habit, the prospect will evoke unpleasant sensations of nausea or anxiety in him and discourage the behavior. Since the habit is liable to return as the conditioned aversion to the stimulus object gradually extinguishes, the long-term success of such a treatment program will depend in part upon the availability of other modes of self-fulfillment which are more adaptive and equally reinforcing.

Aversive conditioning has been used mainly with addictions such as alcoholism, narcotics, and smoking and sexual disturbances such as fetishism, homosexuality, and transvestism. Although drug-induced nausea may be appropriate to establish an aversion toward such things as alcohol because both involve oral ingestion processes, electric shock is generally preferred for other problems because it is easier to work with: whereas drugs require some time to take effect and the effect varies over time, shock can readily be turned on and off and the magnitude reliably controlled. The aversive stimulation may be administered in relation to either the actual objects or situations associated with the maladaptive behavior (alcohol, taverns, cigarettes, or fetishistic sexual objects), or while the person is imagining the objects or situations. The standard procedure reported by Wolpe and Lazarus (1966) consists of attaching the electrodes to the patient's left forearm and using a shock level slightly higher than that which the patient experiences as distinctly unpleasant. The shock is then presented concurrently with the real or imagined stimulus. It is reportedly most effective to conduct the treatment to the point of overlearning, preferably on a daily basis with at least 20 aversion pairing trials per session.

Aversion therapy should always be preceded by a careful diagnostic assessment to make sure the subject is not generally a highly anxious or behaviorally disordered person. In such cases, the use of aversive stimulation has been occasionally found to make the subject more anxious without helping the target behavior. This would be particularly true when the target behavior represents a response to anxiety, for then the introduction of aversive stimuli would be expected to elevate the general anxiety level and perhaps thereby increase the probability of the undesired response (Eysenck, 1960). For example, if a person tends to resort to alcohol when he finds himself feeling tense or anxious, and then electric shock is used to treat this tendency, the administration of shock may increase his anxiety and thereby increase his inclination to drink.

Aversive conditioning has been used in conjunction with a technique known as *anxiety-relief conditioning* in treating homosexuality, transvestism, and other behavioral disorders (Thorpe, Schmidt, Brown, and Castell, 1964). Anxiety-relief conditioning is based on the principle that if a noxious stimulus is endured for several seconds and is then stopped when a specified signal is presented, the relief feelings that accompany the end of the noxious stimulus may become conditioned to this signal. The signal, if something as simple as a word, may then be used independently by successfully conditioned subjects to calm themselves in disturbing life situations. When used in combination with aversive conditioning, it forms the method known as *aversion-relief therapy.* For the treatment of homosexuality, for example, the patient is first given a painful shock in the presence of a homosexual image on a screen. A heterosexual picture is then flashed on the screen at the same time the shock ceases. Thus, homosexual associations become anxiety-evoking and result in avoidance responses, while heterosexual stimuli become conditioned to anxiety-relief and result in approach responses.

The following case, adapted from Lazarus (1960), illustrates the use of aversion-relief procedures:

Since he had learned to walk, the ten-year-old patient had made a habit of waking up and going to his mother's bed in the very early hours of the morning. The child automatically awoke between 1 AM and 2 AM and would immediately go to his mother's bed, an assortment of punishments, threats, bribes, and rewards each having failed to modify this behavior. The patient indicated that, although he was highly motivated to sleep in his own bed, when he awoke anxiety would increase so that he would become panic-stricken unless he entered his mother's bed. The child's behavior was also seriously disrupting the interpersonal relationships in the home.

An aversive stimulus in the presence of the obsessional object was expected to produce a persistent avoidance reaction to the object, and, conversely, approach responses would be conditioned to a stimulus repeatedly presented at the moment of termination of the aversive stimulus. Consequently, the treatment consisted of attaching zinc electrodes to the child's left forearm and instructing him to imagine himself in his mother's bed and to say the words "Mother's bed" as soon as he had a clear image of the situation. A mild electric shock was then delivered to his forearm. The child was told to say "my bed" when he could no longer tolerate the shock (usually about three seconds) at which point the current was immediately switched off. This procedure was repeated 14 times in a ten-minute period.

A week later the patient reported with great pride that he had slept in his own bed every night. Although he had awakened as usual for the first five nights, he had merely "turned over and gone back to sleep." He had slept right through the sixth night, and later reports revealed that he had slept in his own bed for over six months. Furthermore, the patient's ability to remain in his own bed had completely altered numerous adverse environmental pressures, including parental and sibling relationships. The treatment thus appeared to have widespread and positive repercussions on diverse areas of the child's personality [pp. 119–120].

The use of noxious stimulation in aversion therapy is somewhat unpleasant for the therapist as well as the client. If a behavior problem could be treated as effectively and efficiently by some other method which is less discomforting to the client, such an arrangement would certainly be preferred to aversion therapy. One approach to increase the convenience and reduce the distastefulness of aversive conditioning is to use aversive imagery rather than actual noxious stimulation. This method, called *covert sensitization* (Cautela, 1966), requires that the client vividly imagine negative consequences of his behavior. For example, the alcoholic patient may be instructed to imagine himself drinking an alcoholic beverage and then to imagine himself getting nauseous and throwing up the drink.

The following case of a 14-year-old fetishist, adapted from Kolvin (1967), illustrates the use of covert sensitization or *aversive imagery therapy,* as Kolvin calls it:

The boy was charged with indecent assault on three women, and it was suspected that he had committed similar offenses which other victims had not reported. His description of the acts suggested that they were essentially unplanned. On certain occasions when he saw a young woman wearing a skirt, he would be overcome by a kind of trembling and other emotions which he did not have the language to describe; he would feel compelled to run after her and put his hand up under her clothes. He would then run away trembling with exhilaration, excitement, and fear.

At the clinic he revealed himself to be a serious-minded person, pleasant but shy, timid, reserved, and verbally unforthcoming. He reluctantly admitted to anxiety and guilt about his frequent masturbation and also reported a number of frightening dreams. During the course of the early interviews the boy denied any psychosexual knowledge. His problems were explored with him using a psychotherapeutic approach but progress was limited. This was thought to be due to the boy's dullness and inaccessibility. He remained plagued by the urge to commit the above-mentioned acts. At this stage it was decided to decondition him with an aversive stimulus.

The patient's help was enlisted in drawing up a list of "dislikes" which consisted of situations or experiences which were unpleasant for him. The only use made of this list was to ascertain the maximum noxious stimuli, which for him was falling in his dreams and looking down from a precarious situation or from a great height. It was decided to use this unpleasant falling experience from his dreams as the noxious stimulus. In addition, an attempt was made to ascertain the precise fetishist situation.

Thereafter, the patient was taken into a darkened consulting room where he reclined on a couch and closed his eyes. He was encouraged to conjure up imagery according to a story related by the therapist. Empirically it was found that vivid imagery was more easily produced when the adolescent was in a relaxed state. A colorful story of the crucial event was now presented and the patient was asked to visualize accordingly. By careful observation of motor tension, breathing, expression, and so on, it became apparent when the patient was just becoming affectively excited. At this stage the aversive image was introduced in a suggestive and vividly descriptive manner. The response was immediate and mainly reflected in the patient's expression of distaste. In this way the full erotically toned course of events was truncated and the sequence of events unpleasantly anticlimaxed.

Seven half-hour sessions were undertaken on an outpatient basis over a period of three weeks, with two to four trials per session. The treatment was supplemented by an exposition of the biology and psychology of normal sexual behavior, and simple explanations, reassurance, and indications of how to advance towards achieving socially acceptable heterosexual relationships. Towards the end of therapy the mother reported that the boy was more approachable, less difficult,

127

and less inclined to sulk. The probation officer who had known him for some time claimed that there was some evidence of "a growing maturity." The boy denied experiencing any further compulsive urges. A follow-up revealed one incident in which he had "stupidly" accused a neighbor's wife of an illicit affair, but 17 months after the completion of treatment he was reportedly working and apparently quite well [pp. 245–247].[2]

Most reports on the effectiveness of aversion therapy have come from clinical settings, although there have also been several attempts at experimental evaluation. It is not uncommon to find that some patients treated successfully by aversive conditioning methods relapse within several months, although this problem has been reduced by periodical supplementary sessions after the basic treatment is concluded. Rachman and Teasdale (1969a) reported that the approach has been used primarily for the treatment of sexual disorders, of which selected types appear to respond well, and for the treatment of alcoholism, which appears to respond only moderately well. However, they also point out that disorders such as these have proven very resistant to traditional treatment approaches, so even moderate success with aversive conditioning may represent considerable progress. Aversive contingencies will continue to be used clinically until more effective and less unpleasant substitutes for this approach are developed. It may turn out that aversion therapy will prove to be the preferred treatment for certain behavioral problems.

Issues to Consider

1. Three methods of introducing aversive consequences to suppress undesirable instrumental behavior were described in this chapter: noxious punishment involves the presentation of a negative stimulus, response cost involves the removal of a positive reinforcer, and time-out involves the temporary isolation of the subject from all sources of positive reinforcement. We would probably not expect each of these methods of punishment to be equally efficient and effective in all situations. Try to recall instances when your parents

[2]Adapted from *Behaviour Research and Therapy,* 1967, **5,** 245–248. Copyright 1967 by Pergamon Press. Used by permission.

used punishment tactics to control your behavior. Which methods appeared to work best in which situations? Why?

On the basis of this analysis and your knowledge of learning principles, can you formulate any general guidelines for selecting punishment methods to suppress behavior in different situations?

2. On first impression, the theoretical rationale underlying classical aversive conditioning seems fairly logical: the probability of a particular maladaptive response is likely to decrease if its stimulus object is repeatedly associated with negative stimulation. Closer inspection, however, suggests that the process may be somewhat less clear. In order for the treatment to be successful, the bad habit must be suppressed in the person's real-life environment. Yet the noxious stimulus is ordinarily presented only in the treatment setting, and surely the subject knows this. Then why does the subject not give in to his craving for a drink or a cigarette when he knows he will not get shocked for his behavior?

The common explanation is that, by virtue of the repeated pairings with aversive stimuli in the office, unpleasant sensations become classically conditioned to the behavior and its objects. Subsequent inclinations toward the behavior will then evoke these unpleasant sensations regardless of the setting or the person's awareness of the contingencies. This seems reasonable, but note that it assumes the classically conditioned connections between the behavior and the unpleasant associations to be inevitable and relatively immune to cognitive control. If this is so, why is it that the unpleasant associations resulting from shock or emetic drugs do not also become conditioned to related aspects of the behavior and the situation (Sherman, 1971)? In other words, why doesn't the treated alcoholic become somewhat repulsed by drinking other beverages also and the obese person become repulsed by all eating? As another example, why didn't the boy who was treated for going to his mother's bed during the night learn to avoid "Mother" as well as "Mother's bed," since the two were inseparable in terms of the problem?

It would appear inconsistent to explain the reduction of the bad habit entirely in terms of classical aversive conditioning, and then to appeal to cognitive factors in explaining why the aversiveness (fortunately) does not generalize to related behaviors and situations. Can you think of another explanation for the treatment which circumvents this inconsistency?

3. Related to the above issue, what is aversive conditioning's effect upon the individual's attitudes toward the therapist and the treatment setting? Would you expect that the entire therapy situation would evoke an aversion reaction in the client—might he learn to avoid therapy because he gets shocked just as he learns to avoid alcohol because he gets shocked?

Referring to the case of the boy running to his mother's bed, it was reported that during the week following the boy's aversion therapy session, "Although he had awakened as usual for the first five nights, he had merely 'turned over and gone back to sleep.'" It would be interesting to know to what extent it was the conditioned aversiveness associated with "Mother's bed" which led him to go back to sleep, and to what extent he may have (appropriately) feared that if he did go to mother's bed he would be brought in for more aversive therapy sessions. In other words, perhaps the aversiveness of the treatment outweighed the attractiveness of mother's bed.

4. Another issue related to the mechanisms underlying aversive conditioning is motivation. In some cases, such as the overweight woman or the chain-smoking man, the person may be highly motivated to control the bad habit because of its threat to his personal health and appearance; his participation in treatment would be entirely voluntary. With children, a parent ordinarily decides that the problem warrants treatment, and the child may not agree that it is for his own good. In the case of institutionalized adults who are referred by public authorities for treatment of antisocial or criminal behaviors, the person may be required to submit to the treatment entirely against his will. What effects do you think these varying degrees of motivation for therapy might have on the treatment's outcome?

To the extent that the results of aversive conditioning depend only on the pairing of the undesired behaviors with noxious stimuli, the motivation of the subject might be irrelevant provided he attends treatment sessions. On the other hand, if some of the effects depend on cognitive factors and the willing cooperation of the client, the prognosis might not be good for involuntary subjects. Do you think the treatment of involuntary subjects poses any more of a problem for aversion therapy than for other treatment approaches?

5. The situation of involuntary subjects, aside from the added difficulties of treatment, also raises issues related to the ethics of requiring people to undergo treatment. Do you think it is proper for certain authorities to have the power to impose aversive conditioning upon an unwilling person, such as a prison inmate convicted of a sexual offense or an institutionalized drug addict?

If you do not believe this is ethical, would your view be any different if the treatment did not involve noxious stimulation?

If you are ethically opposed to any involuntary treatment of behavior problems, even if these behaviors represent a danger to society, do you have any other suggestions for how such problems might be dealt with more appropriately?

6. Both systematic desensitization for phobic reactions and covert sensitization for maladaptive habits rely on imagery to evoke representations of the problem situations as well as relevant affective responses. Systematic desensitization attempts to arouse positive feelings (relaxation, safety, comfort) in conjunction with images of fear and avoidance situations, and covert sensitization attempts to arouse negative feelings (pain, nausea, anxiety) in conjunction with images of pleasurable activities and situations; one method attempts to reduce fear and aversion, the other to induce fear and aversion. Some advantages and disadvantages of using imagery were considered in earlier chapters on desensitization methods. How might these analyses have implications for covert sensitization?

CHAPTER 11

Self-Control
Methods

Most of the methods of behavioral modification we have considered concern treatment of a behavioral problem by a therapist. The individual has some problem, and he either comes or is brought to the therapist for assistance in overcoming it. There are certainly more than enough existing behavioral difficulties to keep all practitioners constantly busy. This clinical manpower shortage is one factor which has prompted interest in trying to teach self-control methods. If individuals can be taught to control their unrealistic anxieties and depressive feelings and cope more effectively in stressful situations, this may prevent future behavioral problems, thus making for psychologically healthier individuals and a healthier society. Likewise, if individuals can be taught to treat themselves when they develop psychological problems, they can overcome their difficulties without extensive professional assistance.

Although the self-control methods to be considered here generally require some initial training, the long-term objective is to teach the individual to cure himself of present psychological problems and to prevent the development of future ones. The basic principles of learning are presumably the same whether the therapist or the individual himself arranges the treatment contingencies. Therefore, the individual may be taught to be his own therapist in administering certain behavior modification methods we have already described; for example, he may desensitize himself from a phobic reaction or use aversive conditioning to rid himself of a bad smoking habit. On the preventive side, skills such as self-relaxation and interpersonal expressiveness may enable one to become more behaviorally effective and reduce the chances of his developing psychological difficulties. In either case, we attempt to teach the individual self-controlling responses which he may use to control the probability of other responses, either adaptive or maladaptive. This formulation, presented by Cautela (1969), was further illustrated by him as follows:

> It can be said of a heavy drinker, for instance, that he lacks self-control because he is not able to make responses to reduce the frequency of his drinking behavior. A student who says he just can't make himself sit down and study is simply not able to increase the frequency of study responses (i.e., sitting at his desk and reading a text). In other words, he has no self-control in that situation. If an obese individual is presented with great amounts of delectable food at a party but eats little or none of the food, observers at the party may remark that, at the moment, the obese person is exerting good self-control. In each of these examples, self-control is conceptualized as the response of an organism made to control the probability of another response [p. 324].[1]

We shall now consider how certain behavior modification methods, including some described in previous chapters, may be self-administered by a person to treat his own problems, and we shall also consider additional methods of self-control which can help prevent the development of future problems.

[1]In C. M. Franks (Ed.), *Behavior Therapy: Appraisal and Status.* Copyright 1969 by McGraw-Hill, Inc. Reprinted by permission of McGraw-Hill Book Company.

Self-Relaxation

Many people suffer from excessive tension or anxiety, as manifested in basically two ways: some experience high levels of tension most of the time so that they generally appear on edge or uptight, and others tend to get overly upset in response to specific stressful or challenging situations so that they are unable to cope effectively with them. Since tension and relaxation are somewhat opposite both physically and psychologically, if a person can learn to relax himself, this might enable him to reduce residual tension and increase his ability to control anxiety under stress so that adaptive behavior is not disrupted. Jacobson (1938) and Schultz and Luthe (1959) have reported lengthy programs of intensive relaxation training in successfully treating clinical patients.

In the self-relaxation procedure based on the work of Jacobson (1938), the subject is initially instructed to tense and relax alternately specific muscle groups while paying close attention to the muscular changes. This tension–release technique enables him to learn to discriminate feelings of tension and relaxation in his muscles and to let go and relax them more and more deeply. Auxiliary techniques, such as imagining oneself in personally relaxing situations or concentrating on breathing, may be used to further deepen relaxation. Often training will also be provided in the differential relaxation of nonessential muscles while engaged in particular activities. With practice, the subject learns to relax all areas of his body, separately or together, without first having to tense them. Eventually, the well-trained subject can control the experience of tension or anxiety by switching on at will the opposing state of deep muscular relaxation.

Self-relaxation is best learned in a quiet setting with dimmed lights and a comfortable bed or reclining chair. The specific instructions may be presented to oneself through a tape-recording prepared in advance or a professional do-it-yourself relaxation record. The following instructions on the relaxation of the facial area, taken from Wolpe and Lazarus (1966), illustrate the basic tension–release procedure:

> Let all your muscles go loose and heavy. Just settle back quietly and comfortably. Wrinkle up your forehead now; wrinkle it tighter.... And

now stop wrinkling your forehead, relax and smooth it out. Picture the entire forehead and scalp becoming smoother as the relaxation increases. . . . Now frown and crease your brows and study the tension. . . . Let go of the tension again. Smooth out the forehead once more. . . . Now, close your eyes tighter and tighter . . . feel the tension . . . and relax your eyes. Keep your eyes closed, gently, comfortably, and notice the relaxation. . . . Now clench your jaws, bite your teeth together; study the tension throughout the jaws. . . . Relax your jaws now. Let your lips part slightly. . . . Appreciate the relaxation. . . . Now press your tongue hard against the roof of your mouth. Look for the tension. . . . All right, let your tongue return to a comfortable and relaxed position. . . . Now purse your lips, press your lips together tighter and tighter . . . Relax the lips. Note the contrast between tension and relaxation. Feel the relaxation all over your face, all over your forehead and scalp, eyes, jaws, lips, tongue and throat. The relaxation progresses further and further . . . [p. 178].

Wolpe (1958) used a shortened version of Jacobson's progressive relaxation to counteract the anxiety evoked by visualizations of mildly threatening situations in his systematic desensitization treatment for phobic reactions (see Chapter Five of this book). This suggested the possibility that short-term training may be adequate to acquire basic relaxation skills. Some support for this was provided in a study by Paul (1969c), who found decreases in physiological arousal and subjective distress within one to two sessions of training in progressive relaxation. A brief form of Schultz and Luthe's autogenic relaxation training was also found helpful in treating insomnia according to subjects' reports in a study by Kahn, Baker, and Weiss (1968).

I found some evidence in a research study on aquaphobia (portions of which were described on pp. 57–58 and 85–86 of this book) that brief training in self-relaxation may be sufficient to promote certain improvements in a person's well-being and ability to cope with stressful situations (Sherman, 1969; 1972). It will be recalled that 54 female college students received one of six behavioral treatment combinations designed to reduce their fear of the water. Aside from the aquaphobic improvements, peripheral improvements were evident on ten out of 15 general anxiety and clinical personality measures for all students combined. Additional self-ratings of peripheral improvement were highest in those students who had received relaxation training as part of their treatment experience, with 69 percent reporting some specific area of benefit unrelated to the water. The personal reports attributed most such benefits to the ability to relax in stressful situations, such as while delivering a speech, going to sleep at night, or taking an examination.

Another study was then conducted (Sherman and Plummer, in press, 1973) to evaluate further the specific and general effects of self-relaxation. Nine male and 12 female student volunteers received individual training in relaxation over a six-week period by two instructors. The training program was divided into several stages beginning with the tension–release technique and progressing to advanced deepening techniques and training in differential relaxation. Most of the trained students reported in post-treatment assessments that they had acquired basic relaxation skills and had used them to personal advantage. The students' own examples indicated that the training had been especially useful in helping them to recognize and control tension, to go to sleep, and to counteract anxieties related to specific social situations involving evaluation, such as examinations and interviews. Although the trained students also showed more improvement on measures of general anxiety than did twelve male and twelve female control students who had not been trained in relaxation, the differences were not great. It was concluded that, in well-functioning people, relaxation may be useful primarily as a behavioral self-management skill for controlling tension and reducing anxiety in specific stressful situations.

The complexity of modern society and its demands on the individual has precipitated an increased dependence on tranquilizing drugs and other maladaptive crutches. Self-relaxation training, if found to promote behavioral improvements through reduced residual tension and increased tolerance for stress, could afford an efficient and pleasant means of giving the individual greater adaptive control over his affective experience without the threat of adverse consequences.

Self-Desensitization

Systematic desensitization, intended for treating phobic reactions, has been adapted for purposes of self-administration. Migler and Wolpe (1967) successfully used *automated self-desensitization* in the treatment of public speaking anxiety. Their report is adapted here:

> What most immediately brought the patient for treatment was his inability to attend an important staff meeting at work as a result of his fear of public speaking. On past occasions the patient had sometimes spoken in public but always with varying degrees of anxiety. Desensitization was selected as the appropriate treatment for the case, and an anxiety hierarchy was formulated. Representative items were: "sitting in the conference room before anyone else has arrived" (weak item); "people are being called on to speak in turn according to where they are sitting, and there are five speakers ahead of you" (medium item); "two people laugh openly at what you are saying" (strong item).
>
> A specially modified tape-recorder was used to carry out the relaxation and desensitization procedure, the tape having been prepared using the patient's own voice. A further innovation included having the patient administer the desensitization sessions to himself at home without the presence of the therapist. Seven such sessions were required to achieve desensitization to all scenes in the hierarchy.
>
> A week after the final session the patient attended a staff meeting, was called upon to speak, and delivered a long speech disagreeing with all the previous speakers. He experienced no anxiety—in fact, he felt elated and proud of himself. He subsequently found that the desensitization had generalized to other public speaking situations and that now they caused little or no anxiety. In an eight-month follow-up the patient reported that he was continuing to speak in public without anxiety or avoidance behavior [pp. 133–134].[2]

Kahn and Baker (1968) performed a study to compare the effects of conventional desensitization individually administered by therapists in the laboratory to do-it-yourself desensitization self-administered at home. The 16 subjects were college students with a variety of mild phobias. The do-it-yourself kit consisted of a manual and a long-playing record which included relaxation instructions and the framework for a desensitization session. The only therapist contact for the do-it-yourself subjects consisted of an initial interview and a weekly progress-check phone call. On the basis of telephone interviews held about three months after the completion of therapy,

[2]Adapted from *Behaviour Research and Therapy,* 1967, **5**, 133–135. Copyright 1967 by Pergamon Press. Used by permission.

11 of the 13 subjects who completed the program reported some improvement, with the two treatment conditions appearing equally effective. Although the findings are difficult to interpret because of the reliance upon self-reports of improvement, the study nevertheless demonstrates another possible way of arranging for the self-administration of a behavioral treatment.

The theoretical rationale for the desensitization treatment relies primarily on graded exposure to the feared situations in the absence of excessive tension or anxiety (sometimes facilitated by the use of incompatible responses such as relaxation). If this formulation is valid, the presence of a therapist would be unnecessary except to explain the method and perhaps monitor progress. With adequate instruction and materials, the client should be able to learn the methods of self-relaxation, construct an anxiety hierarchy, and arrange for the graded exposure in imagery or reality to the feared situations. Although few attempts have been reported, most methods of imaginal and real-life desensitization would appear to be adaptable for purposes of self-administration.

Exaggerated-Role Playing

Expressive training methods, intended to help an individual overcome interpersonal anxieties and develop effective interpersonal skills, are generally complex and require the participation of a talented therapist. Once having developed increased social competence, however, the individual is more likely to achieve interpersonal successes and less likely to develop psychological problems associated with human relations. In this sense, then, the expressive training may have given the individual some preventive self-control skills which will be useful to him in the future, well after the difficulties which prompted his treatment have been overcome.

One expressive training method, unlike most others, appears to require little special training and can be easily used by many people to perform more effectively in threatening situations. This self-control method, called *exaggerated-role playing* (Wolpe and Lazarus, 1966), consists of instructing the individual to adopt a prescribed role which, unlike his usual behavior, would be more adaptive in a particular situation. He is asked to imagine himself as some other person whose status and interpersonal effectiveness would make him master of what, for the patient, would otherwise be a frustrating situation. He is then told to attempt to behave as though he were such a person the next time he encounters the situation. The following case reported by Lazarus (adapted from Wolpe and Lazarus, 1966) may help to clarify the procedure:

> The patient, a 22-year-old student, complained that he always felt extremely awkward and ill at ease when dining at his girl friend's house. On some occasions his mouth had become so dry that he choked on his food. He was instructed more or less as follows:
> "The next time you dine at her house I want you to act as if you were a wealthy and important businessman, not 22-year-old Peter. As you sit at the table, I want you to look at each person and see him as you think he would appear in the eyes of this mature and wealthy businessman."
> In this case the prescribed role, summating, perhaps, with the subsequent eating responses, served to inhibit the patient's anxieties. After one performance of this exaggerated role he reportedly experienced no further anxieties in that situation [p. 134].

Of course, it is possible that Peter never again experienced anxieties in that situation because he was never invited back. Or, perhaps when Peter viewed his girl friend through the eyes of a mature person, he decided never to go back. In any case, once the person learns this method of behaving effectively as though he were someone else, he can use it in any situation in which he can imagine and mirror the behavior of an appropriate model.

Negative Practice

The method of *negative practice,* also called *massed practice,* may sometimes be used to control one's involuntary motor habits, such as tics, habitual typing errors, or stammering. In this method, the person is required to perform the unwanted response repeatedly to the point of exhaustion so that a high degree of fatigue is produced and the response gradually weakens (Dunlap, 1932). Although the precise basis for the beneficial effects of negative practice is unclear, one possibility is that the effectiveness resides in the accumulation of fatigue-type inhibition (Beech, 1960). Another possibility is that "negative practice succeeds in breaking up habits by making conscious and deliberate the steps involved in their execution [Eysenck, 1960, p. 193]," as for example, conscious attention to the follow-through of the tennis racket or the swing of the golf club may disrupt the performance of these otherwise habitual acts. The fact that the response repeated in negative practice of a motor habit usually only approximates the actual involuntary response adds further to the difficulty of accounting for the effects of the technique.

The following case reported by Lazarus (adapted from Wolpe and Lazarus, 1966) illustrates the successful use of negative practice in the treatment of bruxism, an involuntary grinding of the teeth usually occurring during sleep:

> The patient, a 26-year-old female, was treated for a severe and chronic case of bruxism by the technique of massed practice. She was instructed to grind her teeth nonstop for one minute, then to rest for one minute, and to repeat this procedure five times per trial. She was required to undergo six trials daily for approximately two and one-half weeks.
>
> At the end of this period her husband reported that involuntary gnashing of her teeth, which had occurred mainly while she was asleep, was no longer present.
>
> At a follow-up after almost a year, the woman's improvement had been maintained [p. 136].

Self-Study and Thought Suppression

In their learning theory analysis of psychodynamic formulations, *Personality and Psychotherapy* (1950), Dollard and Miller described two approaches one might follow in attempting to control his own behavior. The first approach, which derives from the psychoanalytic technique of free association, is called *self-study*. This is intended to help an individual resolve real-life conflicts which do not appear on their way to solution after ordinary deliberation—for example, marital conflicts, job difficulties, or misunderstandings with friends. In essence, the individual is required to play the role of both patient and therapist, first by writing down all his thoughts and feelings in relation to the problem, and then by analyzing the material in an attempt to achieve greater insight and understanding into its nature and possible resolution.

According to Dollard and Miller (1950):

> The same rules prevail as in the condition of free association. The thoughts are written down as they come. The person compels himself to follow the rule relentlessly. He perseveres until tired [p. 439].
>
> The person stops to think instead of rushing into action. He attempts to see where blocks in association point and to decode dreams. He tries to trace vague anxieties to specific problem areas. He tests his reasoning for inconsistencies. He searches for missing units in his verbal series. In the privacy of his own mind, he will attempt to label irrational emotional responses which he is making to persons in his real life. He will try at least to be clear with himself when he is at fault. He wants to act reasonably and therefore he must identify his unreasonable behavior.
>
> Undoubtedly, also, he consoles himself as the therapist would console him. He assures himself there is no punishment for merely thinking. He affirms that he is free "to think anything." If he hits upon a solution of a problem, he then goes into action exactly as he was expected to do by the therapist. If he has been unreasonable, he tries to make amends. If he has been stupidly afraid, he tries responding despite the fear. In short, the mental activity of self-study is designed to produce a more adaptive course of action in real life [p. 437].[3]

Dollard and Miller (1950) provide several illustrative examples of the use of self-study, including one case in which a boy successfully used self-study without the formalities of taking time off or of writing:

> He had invited a girl whom he particularly liked but did not know very well to a formal dance. The girl had declined the invitation but said she would be glad to go to dinner before the dance. Trapped by her suggestion and his attraction to her he had agreed to take her to dinner. The boy found the dinner rough going. He was immediately attacked by a stomach-ache so severe that he thought he would be forced to leave the table. He was thus urgently motivated to under-

[3]Dollard, J., and Miller, N. E., *Personality and Psychotherapy.* Copyright 1950 by McGraw-Hill, Inc. This and all other quotes from the same source are reprinted by permission of McGraw-Hill Book Company.

stand his situation. One of the units learned in his analysis came flying to mind. He recalled that aggression against a woman frequently took gastric form in his case. Could it be that he was angry at the girl, and if so, why? He realized immediately that he was angry and had repressed his anger. He had felt exploited by her suggesting dinner when she could not go with him to the dance. When these thoughts occurred, ones contradictory to them came up also. The girl did not seem like an exploitive type. Maybe she wanted to show that she really liked him. There would, after all, be another dance, so why not ask her then and there for another date. This he did, and she accepted with evident pleasure. The combination of this lack of cause for aggression and hope of the future brought relief; the stomach-ache disappeared.

It is interesting to note that the whole reaction occurred under the cover of a social situation and was invisible to his partner. She could have noted only a change from glumness to spontaneity. The incident shows, however, that units of self-study can be performed swiftly, without formal measures, when the subject has learned well some of the needed responses, and the solution involves chiefly a transfer of these units from past to present situations. Once the stomach-ache was labeled as aggression-produced, the rest of the solution appeared rapidly [p. 443].

The method of *thought suppression* is intended to help an individual confront an urgent mental task when other problems, though preoccupying, are either insoluble or can be postponed. Many frustrating situations are out of one's control—for example, a weather-cancelled sports event or an embarrassing social experience—and there are many tasks which can be delayed—for example, reading a magazine or washing the car. And, of course, many activities requiring extended concentration should be done right away—for example, studying for an exam, memorizing the lines for a part in a play, or preparing a class presentation. Problems arise when the individual is confronted by an important mental task but cannot close his mind to the distraction of other thoughts or preoccupations which are insoluble or less imperative.

According to Dollard and Miller (1950):

In order to suppress a train of thought a person must take his attention off the stimuli which are producing this train of thought and turn his attention to some other cues which produce an incompatible train of thought. The essential activity, therefore, is the freedom to manipulate attention responses [p. 448].

The exact habit to be learned is that of recognizing the urgent task, identifying the tasks which are insoluble or can be postponed, and concentrating attentive responses on the initial stimuli of the urgent problem [p. 451].

It may occasionally be helpful to prepare a list of the various feasible tasks with which one is confronted, and then to rank them in terms of priority. This will help identify the task to be tackled first and will also assure that less urgent tasks will not be forgotten since the list will serve as a future reminder.

Dollard and Miller (1950) suggest that if suppression is to become a strong and useful habit, it must be rewarded like any other habit:

The suppression habit is rewarded in two ways, one immediate and the other delayed. The immediate rewards occur when attention is changed from the futile line of thought to that of the necessary task. As the futile responses drop out, the painful stimuli that they produce drop out and hence reward fixing attention on the useful effort. The person, so to say, stops worrying about what cannot be changed and starts acting on the problem that can be solved. The more remote reward occurs at the time of completion of the urgent task. The motivation which impelled this task disappears when the task is completed. Thus, completing the task is rewarded and all of the responses which made completing the task possible may be reinforced by a complex chain of generalized learned rewards.

Learning theory suggests that this "spread" of the effects of the final reward to the first responses involved in suppression can be enhanced by rehearsing these first steps at the time one is experiencing the final reward. It can be helped by sentences like "I'm glad now that I stopped fretting about that disappointment and forced myself to start concentrating. I want to be sure to remember to do the same thing the next time I'm bothered by a hopeless problem." Some persons appear to learn the suppression habit so strongly that they can switch rapidly, with little loss of effort, from one task to another. They can, as it were, turn their minds off and on [pp. 451–452].

It may be noted that the methods of self-study and thought suppression are somewhat opposite but complementary processes. Both are based on the notion that a person's thoughts or higher mental processes play an important part in controlling his behavior. Self-study helps a person discover where he is, what his alternatives

143

are, what he wants to do, what he ought to do first, and so on. Suppression helps him to eliminate the intrusion of irrelevant trains of thought so he can devote himself fully to the most important task, once it has been identified. Just as it would be inappropriate for a person to suppress his thoughts when he is trying to analyze his situation, so it would be inappropriate for him to free associate once a plan of action has been selected. Self-study and thought suppression are not quite as methodologically systematized as some of the other procedures we have considered, but they do purport to help the person cope with his own behavioral problems; they would therefore seem to qualify as promising approaches to self-control.

Other Self-Control Methods

In his book *Science and Human Behavior* (1953) Skinner described a variety of ways people control their own behavior. He maintained that when one thinks out the solution to a problem, chooses a course of action, and so on, "He controls himself precisely as he would control the behavior of anyone else—through the manipulation of variables of which behavior is a function [p. 228]." In other words, we control our own behavior primarily by controlling the conditions which determine our behavior, and there are several ways this can be done. Most of the following illustrations are adapted from Skinner (1953).[4]

1. *Physical Restraint.* The controlling response may consist of imposing some physical restraint upon the response to be controlled. For example, the person may put his hands into his pockets to keep from fidgeting or biting his nails, or he may hold his nose in order to keep from breathing when he is swimming underwater. A variation on this method consists of changing the situation; for example, a woman may leave most of her pocket money at home in order to limit her purchases at a sale.

[4]Adapted with permission of The Macmillan Company from *Science and Human Behavior* by B. F. Skinner. Copyright © 1953 by The Macmillan Company.

2. *Changing the Stimulus.* One may create or eliminate the occasion for a response by manipulating either an eliciting or a discriminative stimulus. For example, a person may eliminate distracting stimuli by closing doors, drawing curtains, closing his eyes, or putting cotton in his ears. Likewise, he may try to avoid overeating by putting a tempting box of candy out of sight. On the other hand, one may arrange discriminative stimuli to assure that appropriate behavior will be occasioned later at the proper time. For example, a woman may tie a string around her finger or write herself a note to remind herself to purchase bread when she goes out later in the day.

3. *Depriving and Satiating.* A person can to some extent control his behavior by filling (or not filling) the needs which provide the underlying motivations. For example, a man who is planning to go to an all-you-can-eat restaurant in the evening may decide to have an early, light lunch so he will be maximally hungry by dinner time. Likewise, a student may intentionally sleep late in the morning of the day preceding an exam because he expects to study all night and does not want to be too tired.

4. *Manipulating Emotional Conditions.* A person may influence his emotional reactions by manipulating the conditions which evoke the appropriate emotions. For example, a man may reread an insulting letter just before answering it to generate emotional behavior which will enable him to write an effective response. Likewise, the extent of an emotional reaction may be reduced by delaying it, for example, by counting to ten before acting in anger. Undesired emotional behavior may also be prevented by manipulating stimuli which will evoke incompatible responses, for example, a child might bite his tongue to keep from laughing on a solemn occasion.

5. *Using Aversive Stimulation.* Sometimes we may control our behavior by arranging aversive consequences if we do not behave the way we wish. For example, by setting an alarm clock and placing it across the room, a person arranges for a strongly aversive

stimulus from which he can escape only by awakening and getting out of bed to turn it off. Similarly, by announcing a behavioral resolution in the presence of other people, one is more likely to behave accordingly to avoid the unpleasant social disapproval which might be forthcoming if he breaks the resolution.

6. *Drugs.* Drugs are often used by individuals to control their emotions and make them more or less disposed to particular behaviors. For example, tranquilizers may be used to reduce the unpleasant feelings of anxiety and tension, appetizers may be used to stimulate hunger, alcohol may be used to reduce inhibitions, and narcotics may be used to generate euphoric behavior. Since the behavioral effects of particular drugs are often in part dependent upon the person's expectations, when drugs are used for specific purposes of self-control the behavioral consequences may be especially consistent with the person's intentions.

7. *Arranging Reward Contingencies.* An individual may attempt to control his behavior by arranging the contingencies of reinforcement so that positive rewards are made dependent upon the completion of desired patterns of behavior.[5] For example, a student who wants to have lunch, play basketball, and visit his girl friend, but has to complete a lengthy term paper, may decide that he will eat after finishing one-third of the paper, play basketball after he has finished another third of the paper, and see his girl friend after the paper is completed. By making the more probable behaviors (eating, playing basketball, visiting his girl friend) contingent upon completion of the less probable behavior (writing), he increases the probability of the latter. The principle that more probable responses may be used to reinforce less probable ones was formulated by Premack (1965), and has application in controlling the behavior of others as well as in self-control.

8. *Doing Something Else.* A person may keep himself from performing undesired behavior by energetically engaging in some other, incompatible behavior. For example, one can try to avoid

[5]A detailed description of this method is presented by Watson and Tharp (1972).

talking about an unpleasant topic by intentionally talking about something else. Participation in the substitute discussion is reinforced by escape from the aversive stimulation associated with the unpleasant topic. As another example, a person may avoid flinching when receiving an injection by stiffening up his body and holding still.

Other methods of self-control are being explored, some representing self-administered adaptations of established therapeutic procedures, others representing new innovations. For example, certain methods of aversion therapy, such as covert sensitization (Cautela, 1966; see p. 126 of this book), have been taught to clients with instructions to carry out the program of aversive contingencies on their own. Goldiamond (1965) reported on the use of operant self-control procedures in the modification of behavioral difficulties related to marriage, to handwriting, and to studying. Harris (1969) reported a successful treatment program for weight reduction based on the self-control of stimulus conditions and reinforcement contingencies. Meichenbaum and Goodman (1971) described a method involving cognitive modeling and self-instruction in which impulsive children showed improvements in self-control after being trained to talk to themselves about what they were doing.

A comprehensive review of the literature on theories and methods for the self-regulation of behavior is presented in Kanfer and Phillips (1970). Although most of the reported research on self-control appears to consist of case illustrations rather than carefully controlled experiments, the area is fairly new. The further development of effective and efficient methods for training people in behavioral self-management skills is an important challenge; it is certainly one of the most exciting and promising areas of behavior modification.

Issues to Consider

1. As Skinner (1953) points out, "A mere survey of the techniques of self-control does not explain why the individual puts them into effect [p. 240]." For example, it is easy to tell an obese person that he can control his overeating by placing a lock on the refrigera-

tor and opening it only at mealtime. Likewise, it is easy to suggest to a student that he can improve his exam performance by turning on the stereo only after he has studied for two hours. If the person follows these self-control arrangements, the probability of the desired behavior will be increased. But what factors lead him to formulate and adhere to a plan of self-control in the first place?

The incentive for executing a self-control plan would often appear to reside in the aversive consequences of not doing so—for example, being rejected by others if one is overweight, getting a hangover if one drinks too much, failing a course if a term paper is not completed, and so on. These aversive contingencies are generally associated with the natural or social environment and are essentially out of the individual's control. In a sense, then, the ultimate behavioral control would appear to reside primarily in factors which are external to the individual, providing the incentive for him to attempt to control his own behavior accordingly. What are your thoughts about this formulation?

2. The attempt to develop effective methods of self-control might be furthered by analyzing how people already exercise self-control. Few of us are anxiety-ridden, stuttering, nail-biting, forgetful, fat alcoholics with smoker's breath, claustrophobia, and a chronic inability to get out of bed in the morning. We all have our share of problems, but there are also many areas which represent problems for others but in which we are relatively problem-free. Instead of asking the usual question of "What are they doing wrong?" we might ask the self-control question of "What are we doing right?"

What techniques do you use to control your bad habits, to postpone small immediate pleasures and work hard in the hope of greater future rewards, to control your anxiety and not blow your cool in stressful situations, to decide what you are going to do and when you are going to do it?

Perhaps some of your techniques are similar to those described in this chapter and others are relatively novel. But if they work for you, they might work for someone else.

3. Having identified a variety of self-control techniques, the next question is how to teach them to other people. Can you remem-

ber how you first learned some of the self-control techniques you use? Does analysis of your own experience give you any clues as to how similar self-control techniques might be taught to other people?

4. It is not difficult to teach most people the methods of self-relaxation so that they can release the tension in their muscles. However, some well-trained subjects report that they occasionally continue to feel upset and anxious despite deep muscular relaxation. Why do you think this might happen?

One possibility is that anxiety may consist of more than just muscular tension. For example, in some people anxiety is manifested as stomach upset, sweating, or rapid breathing, which may be somewhat independent of muscular tension. When you feel anxious, what does the experience consist of?

How could training in self-relaxation help the person whose anxiety experience consists of more than just muscular tension?

In addition to reducing muscular tension, self-relaxation may help (a) focus the person's attention on his body and away from the bothersome thoughts or experiences which prompted his distress and (b) enhance his self-confidence as a result of his presumed ability to control his unpleasant emotional reactions. What do you think of these possibilities?

5. In discussing the role of the therapist, Wolpe and Lazarus (1966) maintain that "it is of first importance to display empathy and establish a trustful relationship [p. 28]," and this view is also held by many other behavior therapists. On the other hand, claims are made for the effectiveness of self-administered behavioral treatments, such as self-desensitization, in which the therapist plays a minor, distant role. According to the learning principles underlying the various behavioral methods, do you see any theoretical need for the presence of an empathic therapist?

Do you think a trustful relationship between therapist and client is likely to promote or retard progress in a behavioral treatment program?

If you had a problem for which a behavioral treatment seemed applicable, would you prefer to be treated by a therapist or administer the methods yourself under his direction?

SECTION 3

Overview of
Behavior
Modification

CHAPTER 12

Summary of Behavior Modification Methods

Our survey of the theory and practice of behavior modification revealed a wide range of methods intended for the treatment of a variety of behavioral problems. The basic procedures and their behavioral focuses are outlined in the following table. Although this summary is intended to help organize and review the material, it should be recognized as an oversimplification which does not do justice to the complexity of the methods or the skill required for their administration. Behavioral therapy should be based on a thorough functional analysis of the problem behavior in which objectives are specified and the treatment is continually evaluated and adapted to the requirements of the individual case.

Summary of Behavior Modification Methods

Method	Behavioral Focus	Basic Procedure
Operant conditioning and extinction	Deficient or maladaptive patterns of instrumental behavior	Systematic manipulation of reinforcement contingencies to shape and maintain desired responses through reward, sometimes for a large group (token economy), and to extinguish undesired responses through non-reward.
Systematic desensitization	Phobic reactions	Imagination of graded series of feared situations while relaxed.
Variants of imaginal desensitization	Mainly phobic reactions	Desensitization procedures which rely upon imagination of the feared situations.
Group desensitization	Common phobic reactions	Systematic desensitization administered to a group of people with the same fear reaction.
Directed muscular activity	Phobic reactions	Imagination of graded series of feared situations while engaged in muscular activity.
Emotive imagery	Phobic reactions in children	Imagination of affectively positive story incorporating graded series of feared situations.
Imaginal desensitization with drugs	Phobic reactions	Imagination of graded series of feared situations while relaxed by drugs.
Implosive therapy	Mainly phobic reactions	Sustained imagination of the most highly feared situations until anxiety extinguishes.
Real-life desensitization	Mainly phobic reactions	Desensitization procedures which rely on exposure to the feared situations in reality.

154

Method	Behavioral Focus	Basic Procedure
With relaxation responses	Phobic reactions	Exposure to graded series of feared situations while relaxed.
With feeding responses	Phobic reactions in children	Exposure to graded series of feared situations while eating.
With sexual responses	Sexual anxieties and inhibitions	Participation in graded series of sexual activities involving increasing intimacy.
With drugs	Phobic reactions	Exposure to graded series of feared situations while relaxed by drugs, sometimes progressively decreased in dosage (gradual drug withdrawal).
Gradual exposure therapy	Phobic reactions	Repeated exposure to graded series of feared situations.
Social modeling	Teach, weaken, strengthen, or prompt specific behavior patterns	Observation and imitation of others' behaviors demonstrated live or through symbolic representations.
Observational learning effects	Develop new behavior patterns	Observation and imitation of desired behavior patterns demonstrated by another person.
Inhibitory and disinhibitory effects	Strengthen or weaken inhibitions of existing responses	Observation of negative or positive consequences of another person's behavior, sometimes with guided response practice (participant modeling, contact desensitization).
Response facilitation effects	Prompt appropriate behavior patterns	Observations of others' behaviors serve as discriminative stimuli in prompting related behaviors.

155

Method	Behavioral Focus	Basic Procedure
Expressive training	Social inhibitions and inadequacies	Several related procedures including modeling, behavior rehearsal, feedback, and prompting to perform graded series of assertive or expressive behaviors.
Aversion therapy	Undesirable instrumental behaviors or maladaptive habits	Introduction of systematic contingencies involving aversive events or noxious stimuli.
Punishment	Undesirable instrumental behaviors	Suppression of undesired response by contingently introducing a negative stimulus (noxious punishment), removing a positive reinforcer (response cost), or isolating subject from sources of positive reinforcement (time-out); punishment should ordinarily be accompanied by contingencies providing for positive reinforcement of alternative, desirable responses.
Classical aversive conditioning	Maladaptive habits including addictions such as alcoholism, narcotics, and smoking and sexual disorders such as fetishism, homosexuality, and transvestism	Introduction of a noxious stimulus in association with the object or situation connected with the maladaptive habit in order to promote an aversion to the object and reduce habit strength; termination of noxious stimulus may be paired with presentation of alternative, acceptable objects (aversion-relief therapy), and the entire treatment may be conducted in imagery (covert sensitization, aversive-imagery therapy).

Method	Behavioral Focus	Basic Procedure
Self-control methods	Increase personal control over own behavior	Behavioral procedures for the self-treatment of existing problems and the prevention of future problems.
Self-relaxation	Reduce tension and improve performance under stress	Alternate tensing and relaxing of muscle groups, pleasant imagery, breathing techniques, and differential training to promote increased control and depth of relaxation.
Self-desensitization	Phobic reactions	Self-administration of systematic desensitization generally aided by instruction manual and recorded directions for relaxation and desensitization.
Exaggerated-role playing	Social inhibitions and inadequacies	Behaving as though one were another person whose status and skills would enable him to perform effectively in the problem situation.
Negative practice	Involuntary motor habits	Repeated deliberate performance of the unwanted response until the response weakens.

157

Method	Behavioral Focus	Basic Procedure
Self-study	Persistent personal problems or conflicts	Writing down and analyzing all thoughts and feelings related to the problem in an attempt to understand and, through action, resolve it.
Thought suppression	Behavioral inertia despite pressing responsibilities	Identification and performance of most urgent task while suppressing preoccupation with other tasks.
Other self-control methods	Increase personal control over own behavior	Self-manipulation of behavior-controlling variables such as physical restraints, eliciting or discriminative stimuli, deprivation or satiation, emotional conditions, aversive stimulation, drugs, reward contingencies, and deliberate performance of incompatible behaviors.

CHAPTER 13

Behavior Modification in Perspective

The basic therapeutic challenge is to maximize the effectiveness and efficiency of treatment while minimizing the discomfort of treatment to the individual. Claims for the superiority of particular approaches should therefore be based upon evidence of higher improvement rates, increased speed of improvement, and/or decreased client discomfort. A variety of behavior modification methods have been developed within the framework of the psychological model which attempt to meet these objectives by using basic principles of learning theory to change maladaptive behavior. Clinical results on behavioral methods have generally been encouraging in terms of both success rate and efficiency, and some have been further supported by controlled experiments. Unfortunately, the absence of definitive information on the results of other systems of psychotherapy precludes direct comparisons. We hope the favorable outcome reports on behavior modification will prompt clinical researchers of other therapeutic persuasions to examine and assess experimentally the results of their interventions. Adequate evalu-

159

ation of therapy depends on precise identification of the maladaptive behavior, the treatment procedures, and the behavior changes. Only through basic research and comparative studies will it be possible to identify the virtues and weaknesses of existing approaches so that improved methods of psychotherapy may continue to be developed.

Despite the generally favorable results with behavioral methods, much is still to be learned about the procedures and their theoretical foundations, and much room for innovation and further improvement also remains. How are the appropriate procedures selected? What client characteristics may be relevant to the prediction of response to treatment? What are the therapeutically potent aspects of the procedures, and how might they be maximized? How effective is the transfer and stabilization of the therapeutic gains from the treatment setting to the real-life environment, and how might this be further facilitated? Are there any adverse side effects of the procedures, and how might they be minimized? These important questions must be confronted by other systems of psychotherapy as well as behavior modification.

The objective of increasing the effectiveness and efficiency of treatment is a worthy one, and the behavioral notion that this will be facilitated by adapting the therapeutic procedures to the requirements of each individual case certainly seems logical. This does not necessarily challenge the value of other psychotherapeutic approaches. Instead, it suggests that the therapist's overall effectiveness is likely to be increased if he increases the range of useful procedures in his treatment repertoire. Even if some of the present behavior modification methods do not ultimately prove worthy, the behavioral approach will have made a valuable contribution through the impact of its scientific orientation.

There is a curative need to help people who experience psychological problems and disabling stress for which they seek professional assistance. There is also a preventive need to teach relatively well-functioning people the psychological skills which will further reduce their vulnerability to stress and increase their behavioral effectiveness. The development of effective and efficient ways of meeting these challenges depends on the formulation of functional theories of behavior and the execution of controlled experiments. The behavior modification movement has provided an impetus and model for such a scientific research program in the important area of psychotherapy.

SECTION 4

Appendix

Advanced Readings
on Behavior
Modification

The following journals are concerned primarily with clinical and research articles on behavior modification:

Behavior Therapy (1970 on)
Behaviour Research and Therapy (1963 on)
Journal of Applied Behavior Analysis (1968 on)
Journal of Behavior Therapy and Experimental Psychiatry (1970 on)

The following books include collections of reprinted and/or original articles on behavior modification:

Advances in behavior therapy, 1968 by R. D. Rubin and C. M. Franks (Eds.) (1969)
Advances in behavior therapy by R. D. Rubin, H. Fensterheim, A. A. Lazarus, and C. M. Franks (Eds.) (1971)
Behavior modification in clinical psychology by C. Neuringer and J. L. Michael (Eds.) (1970)

Behavior therapy: Appraisal and status by C. M. Franks (Ed.) (1969)
Behaviour therapy and the neuroses by H. J. Eysenck (Ed.) (1960)
Case studies in behavior modification by L. P. Ullmann and L. Krasner (Eds.) (1965)
The conditioning therapies: The challenge in psychotherapy by J. Wolpe, A. Salter, and L. J. Reyna (Eds.) (1964)
Control of human behavior by R. Ulrich, T. Stachnik, and J. Mabry (Eds.) (1966)
Control of human behavior: From cure to prevention by R. Ulrich, T. Stachnik, and J. Mabry (Eds.) (1970)
Experiments in behaviour therapy by H. J. Eysenck (Ed.) (1964)
Research in behavior modification by L. Krasner and L. P. Ullmann (Eds.) (1965)

The following books provide extensive reviews and analyses of the theories, research, and practice of behavior modification:

Learning foundations of behavior therapy by F. H. Kanfer and J. S. Phillips (1970)
Principles of behavior modification by A. Bandura (1969)

The following books emphasize the clinical application of behavioral methods:

Aversion therapy and behaviour disorders: An analysis by S. Rachman and J. Teasdale (1969b)
Behavior modification in child treatment by R. M. Browning and D. O. Stover (1971)
Behavior modification in the natural environment by R. G. Tharp and R. J. Wetzel (1969)
Behavior therapy by A. J. Yates (1970)
Behavior therapy and beyond by A. A. Lazarus (1971)
Behavior therapy techniques: A guide to the treatment of neuroses by J. Wolpe and A. A. Lazarus (1966)
Psychotherapy by reciprocal inhibition by J. Wolpe (1958)
Self-directed behavior: Self-modification for personal adjustment by D. L. Watson and R. G. Tharp (1972)
The practice of behavior therapy by J. Wolpe (1969)
The token economy: A motivational system for therapy and rehabilitation by T. Ayllon and N. Azrin (1968)

References

Agras, W. S. Transfer during systematic desensitization therapy. *Behaviour Research and Therapy,* 1967, **5**, 193–200.

Ayllon, T., & Azrin, N. *The token economy: A motivational system for therapy and rehabilitation.* New York: Appleton-Century-Crofts, 1968.

Bandura, A. Social learning through imitation. In M. R. Jones (Ed.), *Nebraska symposium on motivation, 1962.* Lincoln: University of Nebraska Press, 1962.

Bandura, A. *Principles of behavior modification.* New York: Holt, Rinehart & Winston, 1969.

Bandura, A. Psychotherapy based upon modeling principles. In A. E. Bergin & S. L. Garfield (Eds.), *Handbook of psychotherapy and behavior change: An empirical analysis.* New York: Wiley, 1971.

Bandura, A., Blanchard, E. B., & Ritter, B. The relative efficacy of desensitization and modeling approaches for inducing behavioral, affective, and attitudinal changes. *Journal of Personality and Social Psychology,* 1969, **13**, 173–199.

Bandura, A., & Walters, R. H. *Social learning and personality development.* New York: Holt, Rinehart & Winston, 1963.

167

Beech, H. R. The symptomatic treatment of writer's cramp. In H. J. Eysenck (Ed.), *Behaviour therapy and the neuroses.* London: Pergamon, 1960.

Blum, G. S. *Psychoanalytic theories of personality.* New York: McGraw-Hill, 1953.

Blum, G. S. *Psychodynamics: The science of unconscious mental forces.* Belmont, Calif.: Wadsworth, 1966.

Boring, E. G. *A history of experimental psychology.* New York: Appleton-Century-Crofts, 1950.

Brady, J. P. Brevital-relaxation treatment of frigidity. *Behaviour Research and Therapy,* 1966, **4,** 71–78.

Browning, R. M., & Stover, D. O. *Behavior modification in child treatment.* New York: Aldine-Atherton, 1971.

Cautela, J. R. Treatment of compulsive behavior by covert sensitization. *Psychological Record,* 1966, **16,** 33–41.

Cautela, J. R. Behavior therapy and self-control: Techniques and implications. In C. M. Franks (Ed.), *Behavior therapy: Appraisal and status.* New York: McGraw-Hill, 1969.

Cooke, G. The efficacy of two desensitization procedures: An analogue study. *Behaviour Research and Therapy,* 1966, **4,** 17–24.

Davison, G. C. Systematic desensitization as a counterconditioning process. *Journal of Abnormal Psychology,* 1968, **73,** 91–99.

Davison, G. C. A procedural critique of "Desensitization and the experimental reduction of threat." *Journal of Abnormal Psychology,* 1969, **74,** 86–87.

Davison, G. C., & Valins, S. Maintenance of self-attributed and drug-attributed behavior change. *Journal of Personality and Social Psychology,* 1969, **11,** 25–33.

Dollard, J., & Miller, N. E. *Personality and psychotherapy.* New York: McGraw-Hill, 1950.

Dunlap, K. *Habits: Their making and unmaking.* New York: Liveright, 1932.

Eysenck, H. J. The effects of psychotherapy: An evaluation. *Journal of Consulting Psychology,* 1952, **16,** 319–324.

Eysenck, H. J. (Ed.) *Behaviour therapy and the neuroses.* London: Pergamon, 1960.

Eysenck, H. J. (Ed.) *Experiments in behaviour therapy.* London: Pergamon Press, 1964.

Fenichel, O. *The psychoanalytic theory of neurosis.* New York: Norton, 1945.

Ferster, C. B., & Skinner, B. F. *Schedules of reinforcement.* New York: Appleton-Century-Crofts, 1957.

Folkins, C. H., Evans, K. L., Opton, E. M., Jr., & Lazarus, R. S. A reply to Davison's critique. *Journal of Abnormal Psychology,* 1969, **74,** 88–89.

Folkins, C. H., Lawson, K. D., Opton, E. M., Jr., & Lazarus, R. S. Desensitization and the experimental reduction of threat. *Journal of Abnormal Psychology*, 1968, **73**, 100–113.

Franks, C. M. (Ed.) *Behavior therapy: Appraisal and status*. New York: McGraw-Hill, 1969.

Friedman, D. A new technique for the systematic desensitization of phobic symptoms. *Behaviour Research and Therapy*, 1966, **4**, 139–140.

Friedman, P. H. The effects of modeling and role-playing on assertive behavior. In R. D. Rubin, H. Fensterheim, A. A. Lazarus, & C. M. Franks (Eds.), *Advances in behavior therapy*. New York: Academic, 1971.

Goldiamond, I. Self-control procedures in personal behavior problems. *Psychological Reports*, 1965, **17**, 851–868.

Hall, C. S. *A primer of Freudian psychology*. New York: World, 1954.

Hamilton, G. V. *An introduction to objective psychopathology*. St. Louis: C. V. Mosby, 1925.

Harris, M. B. Self-directed program for weight control: A pilot study. *Journal of Abnormal Psychology*, 1969, **74**, 263–270.

Haughton, E., & Ayllon, T. Production and elimination of symptomatic behavior. In L. P. Ullmann & L. Krasner (Eds.), *Case studies in behavior modification*. New York: Holt, Rinehart & Winston, 1965.

Hogan, R. A., & Kirchner, J. H. Preliminary report of the extinction of learned fears via short-term implosive therapy. *Journal of Abnormal Psychology*, 1967, **72**, 106–109.

Hogan, R. A., & Kirchner, J. H. Implosive, eclectic verbal and bibliotherapy in the treatment of fears of snakes. *Behaviour Research and Therapy*, 1968, **6**, 167–171.

Jacobson, E. *Progressive relaxation*. Chicago: University of Chicago Press, 1938.

Jersild, A. T., & Holmes, F. B. Methods of overcoming children's fears. *Journal of Psychology*, 1935, **1**, 75–104.

Jones, M. C. The elimination of children's fears. *Journal of Experimental Psychology*, 1924, **7**, 383–390.

Kahn, M., & Baker, B. Desensitization with minimal therapist contact. *Journal of Abnormal Psychology*, 1968, **73**, 198–200.

Kahn, M., Baker, B. L., & Weiss, J. M. Treatment of insomnia by relaxation training. *Journal of Abnormal Psychology*, 1968, **73**, 556–558.

Kanfer, F. H., & Phillips, J. S. *Learning foundations of behavior therapy*. New York: Wiley, 1970.

Kelly, G. A. *The psychology of personal constructs*. New York: Norton, 1955.

Kirchner, J. H., & Hogan, R. A. The therapist variable in the implosion of phobias. *Psychotherapy: Theory, Research and Practice*, 1966, **3**, 102–104.

Kolvin, I. Aversive imagery treatment in adolescents. *Behaviour Research and Therapy*, 1967, **5**, 245–248.

169

Kraft, T., & Al-Issa, I. Behaviour therapy and the recall of traumatic experience—A case study. *Behaviour Research and Therapy,* 1965, **3**, 55–58.

Krasner, L. The operant approach in behavior therapy. In A. E. Bergin & S. L. Garfield (Eds.), *Handbook of psychotherapy and behavior change: An empirical analysis.* New York: Wiley, 1971.

Krasner, L., & Ullmann, L. P. (Eds.) *Research in behavior modification.* New York: Holt, Rinehart & Winston, 1965.

Lang, P. J., Lazovik, A. D., & Reynolds, D. J. Desensitization, suggestibility, and pseudotherapy. *Journal of Abnormal Psychology,* 1965, **70**, 395–402.

Lazarus, A. A. The elimination of children's phobias by deconditioning. In H. J. Eysenck (Ed.), *Behaviour Therapy and the Neuroses.* London: Pergamon, 1960.

Lazarus, A. A. Group therapy of phobic disorders by systematic desensitization. *Journal of Abnormal and Social Psychology,* 1961, **63**, 504–510.

Lazarus, A. A. The results of behaviour therapy in 126 cases of severe neurosis. *Behaviour Research and Therapy,* 1963, **1**, 69–80.

Lazarus, A. A. Crucial procedural factors in desensitization therapy. *Behaviour Research and Therapy,* 1964, **2**, 65–70.

Lazarus, A. A. A preliminary report on the use of directed muscular activity in counter-conditioning. *Behaviour Research and Therapy,* 1965, **2**, 301–304.

Lazarus, A. A. Behaviour rehearsal vs. non-directive therapy vs. advice in effecting behaviour change. *Behaviour Research and Therapy,* 1966, **4**, 209–212.

Lazarus, A. A. *Behavior therapy and beyond.* New York: McGraw-Hill, 1971.

Lazarus, A. A., & Abramovitz, A. The use of "emotive imagery" in the treatment of children's phobias. *Journal of Mental Science,* 1962, **108**, 191–195.

Lazarus, A. A., & Rachman, S. The use of systematic desensitization in psychotherapy. *South African Medical Journal,* 1957, **31**, 934–937.

Leitenberg, A., Agras, W. S., Barlow, D. H., & Oliveau, D. C. Contribution of selective positive reinforcement and therapeutic instructions to systematic desensitization therapy. *Journal of Abnormal Psychology,* 1969, **74**, 113–118.

Lovaas, O. I. *Behavior modification: Teaching language to psychotic children* (sound film). New York: Appleton-Century-Crofts, 1969.

Lovaas, O. I., Freitas, L., Nelson, K., & Whalen, C. The establishment of imitation and its use for the development of complex behavior in schizophrenic children. *Behaviour Research and Therapy,* 1967, **5**, 171–181.

Masters, W. H., & Johnson, V. E. *Human sexual inadequacy.* Boston: Little, Brown, 1970.

McFall, R. M., & Lillesand, D. B. Behavior rehearsal with modeling and coaching in assertion training. *Journal of Abnormal Psychology,* 1971, **77**, 313–323.

McFall, R. M., & Marston, A. R. An experimental investigation of behavior rehearsal in assertive training. *Journal of Abnormal Psychology,* 1970, **76,** 295–303.

Mealiea, W. L., Jr. The comparative effectiveness of systematic desensitization and implosive therapy in the elimination of snake phobia. Unpublished doctoral dissertation, University of Missouri, 1967.

Meichenbaum, D. H., & Goodman, J. Training impulsive children to talk to themselves: A means of developing self-control. *Journal of Abnormal Psychology,* 1971, **77,** 115–126.

Migler, B., & Wolpe, J. Automated self-desensitization: A case report. *Behaviour Research and Therapy,* 1967, **5,** 133–135.

Miller, N. E., & Dollard, J. *Social learning and imitation.* New Haven: Yale University Press, 1941.

Moreno, J. L. *Psychodrama.* Vol. 1. New York: Beacon, 1946.

Moreno, J. L. *Psychodrama.* Vol. 3. New York: Beacon, 1969.

Neuringer, C., & Michael, J. L. (Eds.) *Behavior modification in clinical psychology.* New York: Appleton-Century-Crofts, 1970.

O'Connor, R. D. Modification of social withdrawal through symbolic modeling. *Journal of Applied Behavior Analysis,* 1969, **2,** 15–22.

Paul, G. L. *Insight vs. desensitization in psychotherapy.* Stanford: Stanford University Press, 1966.

Paul, G. L. Insight versus desensitization in psychotherapy two years after termination. *Journal of Consulting Psychology,* 1967, **31,** 333–348.

Paul, G. L. Outcome of systematic desensitization. I: Background, procedures, and uncontrolled reports of individual treatment. In C. M. Franks (Ed.), *Behavior therapy: Appraisal and status.* New York: McGraw-Hill, 1969.(a)

Paul, G. L. Outcome of systematic desensitization. II: Controlled investigations of individual treatment, technique variations, and current status. In C. M. Franks (Ed.), *Behavior therapy: Appraisal and status.* New York: McGraw-Hill, 1969.(b)

Paul, G. L. Physiological effects of relaxation training and hypnotic suggestion. *Journal of Abnormal Psychology,* 1969, **74,** 425–437.(c)

Paul, G. L., & Shannon, D. T. Treatment of anxiety through systematic desensitization in therapy groups. *Journal of Abnormal Psychology,* 1966, **71,** 124–135.

Premack, D. Reinforcement theory. In D. Levine (Ed.), *Nebraska symposium on motivation: 1965.* Lincoln: University of Nebraska Press, 1965.

Rachman, S. Studies in desensitization—II: Flooding. *Behaviour Research and Therapy,* 1966, **4,** 1–6.

Rachman, S., & Teasdale, J. Aversion therapy: An appraisal. In C. M. Franks (Ed.), *Behavior therapy: Appraisal and status.* New York: McGraw-Hill, 1969.(a)

Rachman, S., & Teasdale, J. *Aversion therapy and behaviour disorders: An analysis.* Coral Gables: University of Miami Press, 1969.(b)

Reed, J. L. Comments on the use of methohexitone sodium as a means of inducing relaxation. *Behaviour Research and Therapy,* 1966, **4,** 323.

Rehm, L. R., & Marston, A. R. Reduction of social anxiety through modification of self-reinforcement: An instigation therapy technique. *Journal of Consulting and Clinical Psychology,* 1968, **32,** 565–574.

Ritter, B. The group treatment of children's snake phobias using vicarious and contact desensitization procedures. *Behaviour Research and Therapy,* 1968, **6,** 1–6.

Rubin, R. D., Fensterheim, H., Lazarus, A. A., & Franks, C. M. (Eds.) *Advances in behavior therapy.* New York: Academic, 1971.

Rubin, R. D., & Franks, C. M. (Eds.) *Advances in behavior therapy, 1968.* New York: Academic, 1969.

Salter, A. *Conditioned reflex therapy.* New York: Creative Age, 1949.

Schultz, J. H., & Luthe, W. *Autogenic training.* New York: Grune & Stratton, 1959.

Sherman, A. R. Therapy of maladaptive fear-motivated behavior in the rat by the systematic gradual withdrawal of a fear-reducing drug. *Behaviour Research and Therapy,* 1967, **5,** 121–129.

Sherman, A. R. Therapeutic factors in the behavioral treatment of anxiety. Unpublished doctoral dissertation, Yale University, 1969.

Sherman, A. R. Real-life exposure as a primary therapeutic factor in the desensitization treatment of phobic anxiety. Unpublished paper presented at the meeting of the Western Psychological Association, Los Angeles, April 1970.

Sherman, A. R. Some reflections on behavior modification: Problems, issues, and possible future directions. Unpublished paper presented at the Camarillo Behavior Modification Conference, Camarillo, California, March 1971.

Sherman, A. R. Real-life exposure as a primary therapeutic factor in the desensitization treatment of fear. *Journal of Abnormal Psychology,* 1972, **79,** 19–28.

Sherman, A. R., & Plummer, I. L. Training in relaxation as a behavioral self-management skill: An exploratory investigation. *Behavior Therapy,* in press, 1973.

Sherman, A. R., & Sherman, L. H. Individual and group behavioral modification in the school setting. Unpublished case studies conducted at Hamden, Connecticut, 1967.

Sherman, J. A. Use of reinforcement and imitation to reinstate verbal behavior in mute psychotics. *Journal of Abnormal Psychology,* 1965, **70,** 155–164.

Sherman, J. A., & Baer, D. M. Appraisal of operant therapy techniques with children and adults. In C. M. Franks (Ed.), *Behavior therapy: Appraisal and status.* New York: McGraw-Hill, 1969.

Skinner, B. F. *Walden two.* New York: Macmillan, 1948.

Skinner, B. F. *Science and human behavior.* New York: Macmillan, 1953.

Skinner, B. F. *Contingencies of reinforcement: A theoretical analysis.* New York: Appleton-Century-Crofts, 1969.

Skinner, B. F. *Beyond freedom and dignity.* New York: Knopf, 1971.

Stampfl, T. G., & Levis, D. J. Essentials of implosive therapy: A learning-theory-based psychodynamic behavioral therapy. *Journal of Abnormal Psychology,* 1967, **72,** 496–503.

Tate, B. G., & Baroff, G. S. Aversive control of self-injurious behavior in a psychotic boy. *Behaviour Research and Therapy,* 1966, **4,** 281–287.

Tharp, R. G., & Wetzel, R. J. *Behavior modification in the natural environment.* New York: Academic, 1969.

Thorpe, J. G., Schmidt, E., Brown, P. T., & Castell, D. Aversion-relief therapy: A new method for general application. *Behaviour Research and Therapy,* 1964, **2,** 71–82.

Ullmann, L. P. Making use of modeling in the therapeutic interview. In R. D. Rubin & C. M. Franks (Eds.) *Advances in Behavior Therapy, 1968.* New York: Academic, 1969.

Ullmann, L. P., & Krasner, L. (Eds.) *Case studies in behavior modification.* New York: Holt, Rinehart & Winston, 1965.

Ulrich, R., Stachnik, T., & Mabry, J. (Eds.) *Control of human behavior.* Glenview, Ill.: Scott, Foresman, 1966.

Ulrich, R., Stachnik, T., & Mabry, J. (Eds.) *Control of human behavior: From cure to prevention.* Glenview, Ill.: Scott, Foresman, 1970.

Walker, E. L. *Conditioning and instrumental learning.* Belmont, Calif.: Wadsworth, 1967.

Watson, D. L., & Tharp, R. G. *Self-directed behavior: Self-modification for personal adjustment.* Belmont, Calif.: Brooks/Cole, 1972.

Watson, J. B. *behaviorism.* New York: W. W. Norton & Company, 1930.

Wolpe, J. *Psychotherapy by reciprocal inhibition.* Stanford: Stanford University Press, 1958.

Wolpe, J. The systematic desensitization treatment of neuroses. *Journal of Nervous and Mental Disease,* 1961, **132,** 189–203.

Wolpe, J. The experimental foundations of some new psychotherapeutic methods. In A. J. Bachrach (Ed.), *Experimental foundations of clinical psychology.* New York: Basic, 1962.

Wolpe, J. *The practice of behavior therapy.* New York: Pergamon, 1969.

Wolpe, J., & Lazarus, A. A. *Behavior therapy techniques: A guide to the treatment of neuroses.* New York: Pergamon, 1966.

Wolpe, J., Salter, A., & Reyna, L. J. (Eds.) *The conditioning therapies: The challenge in psychotherapy.* New York: Holt, Rinehart & Winston, 1964.

Wolpin, M., & Raines, J. Visual imagery, expected roles and extinction as possible factors in reducing fear and avoidance behavior. *Behaviour Research and Therapy,* 1966, **4,** 25–37.

Yates, A. J. *Behavior therapy.* New York: Wiley, 1970.

Name Index

Abramovitz, A., 65-67, 170
Adler, A., 5
Agras, W. S., 56, 57, 167, 170
Al-Issa, I., 54-55, 170
Ayllon, T., 42, 44, 166, 167, 169
Azrin, N., 42, 166, 167

Bachrach, A. J., 173
Baer, D. M., 42, 172
Baker, B. L., 135, 137-138, 169
Bandura, A., 91-92, 96-99, 103, 108, 166, 167
Barlow, D. H., 56, 170
Baroff, G. S., 122-123, 173
Beech, H. R., 140, 168
Bergin, A. E., 97, 167, 170
Binet, A., 15
Blanchard, E. B., 97-98, 167
Blum, G. S., 5, 168
Boring, E. G., 14, 168
Brady, J. P., 68, 168
Brown, P. T., 125, 173

Browning, R. M., 166, 168

Castell, D., 125, 173
Cattell, J. M., 14
Cautela, J. R., 126, 133, 168
Cooke, G., 75-76, 168

Davison, G. C., 56, 57, 59, 72-73, 168
Dewey, J., 14
Dollard, J., 91, 140-144, 168, 171
Dunlap, K., 139, 168

Ebbinghaus, H., 14
Evans, K. L., 59, 168
Eysenck, H. J., 10-11, 44, 124-125, 140, 166, 168, 170

Fenichel, O., 5, 91, 168
Fensterheim, H., 165, 169, 172
Ferster, C. B., 35, 168
Folkins, C. H., 59, 168, 169
Franks, C. M., 133, 165, 166, 168, 169, 171, 172, 173

174

Subject Index